D1737046

Table of Contents

Forward

Meals are pockets of happiness—those moments in daily life that help us recharge and rejoice.

In the rush of modern living, we sometimes forget that food is not merely sustenance but a chance to recharge, reconnect, and celebrate life's simplest pleasures. In the Mediterranean, this is understood almost instinctively. It's not about an obsessive focus on the next meal, nor about worrying over every bite. Instead, it's about living a lifestyle that naturally incorporates food as a source of daily delight—a lifestyle that invites you to savor, enjoy, and find contentment in the everyday.

When embracing the Mediterranean lifestyle, slices of joy are woven into everyday life through food, among other simple pleasures. This way of living is for everyone, as everyone deserves to enjoy good food. In a way, this food culture is deeply egalitarian, where everyone, regardless of background, can partake in the simple yet profound pleasure of a well-cooked meal.

But food is more than just joy; it's a canvas for creativity, a way to express ourselves, and to find comfort in the familiar while exploring the new. Cooking, in the Mediterranean sense, is both an art and a narrative—a way to weave inspiration, comfort, and a moment of calm into the story of our lives. The act of preparing a meal becomes a ritual, a time to slow down (even when prepping a quick meal for two), to connect with the ingredients, and to create something that nourishes not just the body but the soul.

It is a creative outlet, a way to distill good substance into the narrative of our lives.

In the Mediterranean, cooking follows an impulsive logic: go seasonal, defy trends, and use what's in the pantry and fridge. More often than not, it starts with a hot pan, a splash of olive oil, and an onion—imperfectly chopped and dancing in the hot oil. Maybe you're dancing along, holding a glass of wine. Nothing is off-limits. It's all about balance—and yes, that includes a glass of wine or a decadent dessert once in a while. Think food, served with a side of lifestyle.

Cooking the Mediterranean way is based on the deeply rooted culinary art of the region, but there's no single right way to cook. You can improvise, and yes, you can have your pie and eat it too. There's a saying in Greece that goes, "You can have your pie and the dog fed," meaning you can have it all—just be ready to hit the unfollow button on perfection and embrace the inherent artistry of the imperfect.

The purpose of each dish is simple: to be eaten, to sustain, and to replenish. Making food grounds us and reminds us of our basic instinct to eat, nourish, and care for our loved ones with the basic act of cooking a homemade meal. This is the Mediterranean narrative.

A Touch of Innovation for Two

The concept of family has evolved significantly over the past few decades, expanding to embrace a broader, more diverse understanding of what it means to belong. When I first envisioned this cookbook, my goal was to create something unique—something that resonates with the spirit of today's families. I wanted to celebrate the variety of connections that define modern life, catering to those who live joyfully on their own terms. Whether it's friends, housemates, couples, relatives, or chosen family, this cookbook is designed for anyone who shares a bond of love and togetherness in all its beautiful forms.

I wanted to move beyond the familiar to represent Mediterranean food in a new light. The Mediterranean cuisine is rich and varied, but I wanted to distill its essence into recipes that are both tantalizing and true to the region yet simple enough to recreate in any kitchen, anywhere in the world.

This cookbook is for two, designed to bring the flavors of the Mediterranean to your table without the hassle of dealing with mountains of leftovers. The recipes are crafted to provide just the right amount—enough to satisfy, to open up these pockets of delicious happiness, but not to overwhelm. And in those instances where leftovers are inevitable, I've made sure they don't go to waste. Instead, they find new life in another recipe, another chapter, transforming what's left into something just as delicious, if not more so.

This book isn't just about cooking—it's about creating experiences. I've carefully selected a variety of ingredients—different sources of carbohydrates, proteins, and fibers—to ensure that there's something for everyone. Each recipe is a small journey, a taste of the Mediterranean that's accessible, enjoyable, and, above all, delicious. But more than just recipes, each chapter in this book comes with a story, because the real purpose of this book is to transport you. Each time you turn a page, I want you to feel like you're escaping to a little corner of the Mediterranean, even if just for a moment.

It's about the joy of discovery, the pleasure of sharing a meal, and the satisfaction of creating something with your own hands. Whether you're an experienced cook or someone just starting to explore the kitchen, these recipes are designed to be approachable yet exciting—a blend of tradition and innovation that captures the spirit of the Mediterranean while also offering something fresh and new.

So, here's to meals that are more than just food, but moments of happiness, of connection, of joy. Here's to cooking with a sense of freedom, of creativity, and of balance. Here's to embracing the imperfections, to finding beauty in the simple, and to savoring every bite. Because in the end, that's what Mediterranean cooking is all about—living life to the fullest, one meal at a time.

CHAPTER 1
GREECE

The Art of 'Toso-Oso'

Welcome to the first chapter of your Mediterranean Escape. In this culinary journey, let's explore the Greek concept of 'toso-oso'—meaning the perfect amount. In Greek culture, this idea is the epitome of balance: not too much, not too little, but simply just enough to achieve the ideal harmony between pleasure, sustenance, and effortless elegance.

Let's paint a picture: Imagine yourself on a Greek island or perhaps perched on a mountain overlooking the Aegean Sea, an ouzo lemonade in hand, savoring a rich, flaky spinach-feta pie that you made yourself with minimal effort using phyllo dough. As you bite into the pie, the flavors transport you straight to Greece, where food is as much about the experience as it is about nourishment. Now take a sip of that ouzo lemonade—you earned it.

And if you find yourself with leftover phyllo dough, don't worry—even though it can't be refrozen, it can certainly be repurposed. I made sure to be very mindful of these little details that minimize waste, making your journey a sustainable one. Take it on a culinary journey to Turkey, where it transforms into crispy Sigara Böreği, making for a super satisfying win-win situation and an excuse for another kitchen adventure tomorrow.

But if tomorrow feels too far away, how about staying in Greece just a little longer and indulging in Baklava cups for two, using up the rest of that phyllo dough and leaving you with full bellies and happy minds. (You will find all these recipes in the next few pages and chapters).

In this book, I loved the idea of infusing true innovation into every chapter, ensuring an out-of-the-box culinary experience throughout. However, when it comes to the Greek chapter, I've taken a slightly different approach. Here, you'll find that I've stayed as true to tradition as possible, with only a few thoughtful adaptations. It felt right to honor the authenticity of Greek cuisine, preserving its timeless flavors while offering just a hint of modern flair. Maybe it's the 'Toso-Oso' that got so deep into my head that I simply can't resist it.

In Greece, food is taken very seriously, yet there's an inherent and undeniably unapologetic playfulness in the way it's approached. The Greeks are addicted to seasonal produce, generously bathed in olive oil.

At the bustling (and sometimes maybe a bit overwhelming) open markets, vendors with sun-kissed skin and weathered dexterous hands sell fruits and vegetables straight from the farmers to your table. People queue up eagerly for the juiciest, plumpy red tomatoes, the freshest, intensely yellow-yolked eggs, and the most fragrant hand-picked oregano, harvested straight from the mountains.

I'll be honest—nothing tastes quite the same as it does when you're actually in Greece. But in this chapter, we'll get you as close to that authentic experience as possible, bringing the essence of Greece to your kitchen.

SALAD

Greek Village Salad

a.k.a Horiatiki (Hor-YAH-tee-kee with emphasis on the second syllable: "YAH" to sound like a true local).

Have you ever heard of the Greek tradition of 'vouta'? It's the act of dipping rustic, crusty bread into the salad juices. Think of it as the Mediterranean version of a high-five! Tear off a chunk of bread, give it a good dunk into those luscious salad juices, and savor the perfect marriage of flavors. It's messy, it's delicious, and it's practically a national pastime. So, get ready to embrace your inner Greek and let your bread have a tasty bath!

Ingredients For Two

- 2 large ripe tomatoes
- 1 medium cucumber
- 1/2 small red onion
- 10-12 Kalamata olives, pitted
- 3.5 oz (about 100g) feta cheese, cut into thick slices or crumbled
- 2 tablespoons extra virgin olive oil
- 1 tablespoon red wine vinegar
- 1/2 teaspoon dried oregano
- Sea salt to taste
- Optional: A few fresh parsley leaves for garnish

✅ **Prepare Time:**

10 Minutes

✅ **Total Time:**

10 Minutes

✅ **Serving:**

2

Instruction

- Wash and cut the tomatoes into wedges. Place them in a large salad bowl.

- Slice the cucumber into rounds and add to the bowl with the tomatoes.

- Thinly slice the red onion and add to the mix. If you prefer a milder onion flavor, soak the slices in cold water for 5 minutes, then drain before adding.

- Scatter the Kalamata olives over the vegetables.

- Crumble the feta cheese on top of the salad. Or dice into thick cubes for a traditional rustic look if preferred.

- Drizzle the olive oil over the salad. Add a splash of red wine vinegar.

- Sprinkle the dried oregano over the salad.

- Season with a pinch of sea salt. Be cautious with the salt, as the feta and olives are already salty.

- Gently toss the salad to combine the ingredients.

- Serve immediately, garnished with fresh parsley leaves if you have them, and with crusty bread on the side.

Tried & True Tips & Hacks

Meal Prepping: Prepare the salad ingredients in advance by chopping the vegetables and storing them in separate airtight containers in the fridge. This way, when you're ready to assemble the salad, everything is prepped and ready to go, saving you valuable time.

Quick Cleanup: Use a large cutting board with compartments or a tray to chop and organize your ingredients. This minimizes mess and makes it easier to transfer the chopped vegetables to your salad bowl.

Leftovers

Repurpose Leftovers: If you have leftover tomatoes, cucumbers, or olives, consider using them in the Souvlaki Bowls recipe or maybe as a topping for a grilled chicken sandwich/ wrap the next day. The flavors will marinate nicely, adding an extra punch to your dish.

Big Jar of Olives? No problem! Take them to Spain (by flipping through a few more pages) and use them up in a delicious Orange and Olive Salad with Smoked Paprika Vinaigrette.

Stale Bread Tip: If you have leftover crusty bread from serving with the salad, cut it into cubes and toast them to make croutons for your next salad.

Cooking Together

Shared Prep: Divide tasks, like chopping vegetables and mixing dressing, to involve both people and speed up preparation.

Personal Touches: Customize the recipe with your favorite ingredients or spice levels to suit both your tastes.

Cooking Playlist: Create a shared playlist to enjoy while cooking, setting a fun and relaxed atmosphere.

APPETIZER
Spanakopita Triangles

Spanakopita is a beloved breakfast staple in Greece, often enjoyed steaming hot from local bakeries on every corner. It's a nostalgic taste that instantly takes you back to childhood, where burning your tongue because you couldn't wait for it to cool was all part of the experience—and totally worth it. I've reimagined this classic into a more refined, adult version by adding fresh herbs for a burst of flavor and earthiness. Perfect as an appetizer for two, this recipe yields 6 triangles—enough for you to enjoy two each as an appetizer and save a couple for a fantastic cold breakfast the next day (preferably served with chocolate milk if you are after the full experience). A little taste of Greece with a grown-up twist.

Ingredients for Two

- 1 tablespoon olive oil
- 1 small yellow or red onion, finely chopped
- 4 cups fresh spinach leaves, chopped
- 1 large garlic clove, minced
- 1/2 cup feta cheese, crumbled
- 1 tablespoon fresh dill, chopped
- 1 tablespoon fresh parsley, chopped
- 1 medium egg, lightly beaten
- 4 sheets of phyllo pastry
- 2 tablespoons extra virgin olive oil (plus extra for brushing)
- Sea salt and pepper, to taste

✓ **Prepare Time:**
20 minutes

✓ **CookTime:**
25 minutes

✓ **Total Time:**
45 Minutes

✓ **Serving:**
2 (Makes 6 triangles)

Instruction

- Heat 1 tablespoon of olive oil in a skillet over medium heat. Add the chopped onion and sauté until softened and translucent, about 3-4 minutes.

- Add the chopped spinach and garlic to the skillet and cook until wilted, about 2-3 minutes. Remove from heat and let cool slightly.

- In a mixing bowl, combine the sautéed spinach mixture, crumbled feta cheese, chopped dill, parsley, and the beaten egg. Season with sea salt and pepper to taste. Mix until well combined.

- Preheat your oven to 350°F (175°C).

- Lay one sheet of phyllo pastry on a clean, flat surface and brush lightly with olive oil. Place another sheet on top and brush with olive oil again. Repeat until you have layered four sheets.

- Place a heaping teaspoon of the spinach-feta filling at the end of each phyllo strip.

- Fold one corner of the phyllo over the filling to form a triangle. Continue folding the triangle over itself, keeping the filling enclosed until you reach the end of the strip.

- Brush the outside of each triangle with a little more olive oil to ensure a golden, crispy finish.

- Place the triangles on a baking sheet lined with parchment paper.

- Bake in the preheated oven for 20-25 minutes or until the triangles are golden brown and crispy.

- Let the spanakopita triangles cool slightly before serving. Enjoy warm, perfect for sharing between two!

Tried & True Tips & Hacks

Keep it Crispy: To maintain the crispiness of your spanakopita triangles, brush each layer of phyllo with just enough olive oil to coat it evenly, but don't overdo it. This ensures a golden, flaky finish.

Perfect Filling: Make sure to cool the spinach mixture before adding the egg and feta. This prevents the filling from becoming too watery and helps the flavors meld beautifully.

Leftovers

Leftover Phyllo? No problem! Any extra phyllo sheets can be wrapped tightly and stored in the fridge for a few days. They're perfect for whipping up another batch of spanakopita or using in the Baklava Cups from this chapter. If you are skipping dessert, you can always make crispy Sigara Böreği, straight from Turkey! Nothing goes to waste!

Next-Day Breakfast: These triangles are just as delicious cold, making them a convenient grab-and-go breakfast for the next day.

Spinach Bonus: Spinach usually comes in large packages, but that's okay. Don't let it go to waste! Use it in the Spanish Tortilla with Spinach and Goat Cheese recipe from the "Spain" chapter for another tasty dish.

Cooking Together

Divide and Conquer: One person can prepare the spinach filling while the other handles the phyllo dough, brushing it with olive oil and layering it. This teamwork speeds up the process and makes it more fun. Folding Fun: Make the folding of the phyllo triangles a shared activity—one person fills, and the other folds. It's a simple task but a great way to collaborate in the kitchen.

Taste Test: As you prepare the filling, both of you can taste and adjust the seasoning together, making sure the flavors are just right before assembling the triangles.

MAIN COURSES
Chicken Souvlaki Bowls

One of the exciting innovations that made the cut in this chapter is this deconstructed souvlaki bowl—a fresh twist on the traditional skewer. Instead of grilling on skewers, I've turned this classic Greek favorite into a complete, customizable meal, served in a bowl with zesty, lemony rice and vibrant vegetables. It's incredibly easy to personalize: swap out the chicken for tempeh or tofu for a vegan version, use vegetable broth in place of chicken broth, and opt for plant-based yogurt in the tzatziki. With this recipe, the sky's the limit for creating your perfect Greek-inspired bowl.

Ingredients for Two

For the Chicken Marinade

- 2 tablespoons extra virgin olive oil
- 2 tablespoons lemon juice
- 2 garlic cloves, minced
- 1 teaspoon dried oregano
- 1/2 teaspoon ground cumin
- 1/2 teaspoon paprika
- Salt and pepper to taste
- 2 boneless, skinless chicken breasts cut into bite-sized pieces

For the Lemony Rice

- 1 cup chicken broth (or water)
- 1/2 cup basmati or jasmine rice
- 1 tablespoon extra virgin olive oil
- 1 tablespoon lemon juice
- 1/2 teaspoon lemon zest
- Sea salt to taste

✅ **Prepare Time:**	20 minutes (plus 30 minutes marinating time)
✅ **CookTime:**	25 minutes
✅ **Total Time:**	45 Minutes
✅ **Serving:**	2

For the Tzatziki

- 1/2 cup Greek yogurt
- 1/2 cucumber, grated and drained
- 1 garlic clove, minced
- 1 tablespoon extra virgin olive oil
- 1 teaspoon lemon juice
- Sea salt and pepper to taste

For the Bowl Assembly

- 1/2 cucumber, sliced
- 1/2 cup cherry tomatoes, halved
- 1/4 cup Kalamata olives, pitted and halved
- Fresh parsley, chopped (for garnish)
- Lemon wedges (for serving)

Instruction

For the Chicken Marinate

- In a bowl, combine olive oil, lemon juice, minced garlic, oregano, cumin, paprika, salt, and pepper.
- Add the chicken pieces and toss to coat well. Cover and marinate in the refrigerator for at least 30 minutes (or up to 2 hours for more flavor).

For the Rice

- In a small saucepan, bring the chicken broth to a boil.
- Stir in the rice, olive oil, lemon juice, lemon zest, and a pinch of salt.
- Lower the heat, cover, and simmer for about 15 minutes or until the rice is tender and has absorbed the liquid.
- Fluff the rice with a fork and set aside.

For the Tzatziki

- In a small bowl, combine Greek yogurt, grated cucumber, minced garlic, olive oil, lemon juice, salt, and pepper. Mix well and refrigerate until ready to use.
- Next up, heat a grill pan or skillet over medium-high heat.
- Add the marinated chicken pieces and cook for 5-7 minutes on each side or until the chicken is cooked through and has nice grill marks.
- Divide the lemony rice between two bowls.
- Top each bowl with grilled chicken, sliced cucumber, cherry tomatoes, and Kalamata olives.
- Add a generous dollop of tzatziki on the side.
- Garnish with chopped parsley and serve with lemon wedges on the side.
- Serve the Chicken Souvlaki Bowls immediately, letting the flavors meld together as you enjoy a fresh, vibrant, and satisfying meal.

Tried & True Tips & Hacks

Quick Marinade Hack: If you're short on time, you can marinate the chicken in a resealable bag, ensuring the marinade coats the chicken evenly. Even a quick 15-minute marinade at room temperature will still impart good flavor.

Rice Perfection: To avoid sticky rice, rinse it under cold water until the water runs clear before cooking. This removes excess starch and helps the rice stay fluffy.

Tzatziki Time-Saver: Make the tzatziki a day ahead to save time. The flavors will meld beautifully, giving you an even more delicious sauce.

Grilling Indoors: If you don't have a grill pan, you can use a regular skillet. To get a smoky flavor, add a dash of smoked paprika to the marinade.

Leftovers

Repurpose Leftover Chicken: Any leftover grilled chicken can be chopped and added to a salad or stuffed into a pita with leftover tzatziki for a quick and tasty lunch.

Rice Reimagined: Use leftover lemony rice to make fried rice. Add some veggies, a beaten egg, and any leftover chicken for a simple, next-day meal.

Tzatziki as a Dip: Leftover tzatziki is perfect as a dip for fresh veggies, pita chips, or even as a sandwich spread.

Creative Toppings: Leftover cucumber, tomatoes, and olives can be added to a basic green salad or used as toppings for a Mediterranean-style pizza.

Spinach Savvy: If you have leftover spinach from the Spanakopita Triangles recipe, use it in a Spanish Tortilla with Spinach and Goat Cheese from the Spain chapter for a quick and easy meal.

Cooking Together

Team Up: One person can marinate the chicken while the other prepares the tzatziki and rice, making the process more efficient.

Customize Your Bowls: As you assemble the bowls, each person can customize their toppings, adding more of their favorite ingredients to suit their taste.

MAIN COURSES
Moussaka for Two

This Moussaka for Two brings a touch of Greece right to your table with a comforting twist on this classic dish. Traditionally enjoyed in Greece but also cherished around the world, this casserole of tender eggplant, savory ground beef, and creamy béchamel evokes nostalgia with every bite. I have refined it into a simple, elegant version perfect for two, ensuring you can savor the richness of this beloved dish without any fuss. For a fun bonus, try the leftover moussaka as a hearty breakfast or transform it into a Mediterranean casserole. With this recipe, you get the taste of Greece and a bit of creative flexibility for any extras!

Ingredients for Two

For the Eggplant

- 1 medium eggplant
- 2 tablespoons extra virgin olive oil
- Sea salt and pepper to taste

For the Meat Sauce

- A splash of extra virgin olive
- 1/2 onion, finely chopped
- 2 garlic cloves, minced
- 1/2 lb ground beef
- 1 can (14.5 oz) diced tomatoes
- 1 tablespoon tomato paste
- 1/2 teaspoon dried oregano
- 1/2 teaspoon ground cinnamon
- 1/4 teaspoon ground allspice
- 1/4 cup red wine (optional)
- Sea salt and pepper to taste

For the Béchamel Sauce

- 2 tablespoons unsalted butter
- 2 tablespoons all-purpose flour
- 1 cup milk
- 1/2 cup grated Parmesan cheese
- 1/4 teaspoon ground nutmeg
- Sea salt and pepper to taste

✓ **Prepare Time:**
20 minutes

✓ **CookTime:**
25 minutes

✓ **Total Time:**
1 hour 5 minutes

✓ **Serving:**
2

Instruction

For the Eggplant

- Preheat the oven to 400°F (200°C).
- Slice the eggplant into 1/4-inch thick rounds.
- Brush both sides of the eggplant slices with olive oil and season with sea salt and pepper.
- Arrange the slices on a baking sheet and roast for 20 minutes, flipping halfway through, until tender and golden brown. Set aside.

For the Meat Sauce

- Heat a skillet over medium heat and add a splash of olive oil.
- Add the chopped onion and cook until softened, about 3-4 minutes.
- Add the minced garlic and cook for another minute.
- Add the ground beef and cook until browned, breaking it up with a spoon.
- Stir in the diced tomatoes, tomato paste, oregano, cinnamon, allspice, and red wine (if using). Season with sea salt and pepper.
- Simmer for 10-15 minutes, until the sauce thickens. Adjust seasoning as needed.

For the Béchamel Sauce

- In a small saucepan, melt the butter over medium heat.
- Whisk in the flour and cook for 1-2 minutes, until it forms a paste (roux).
- Gradually whisk in the milk, making sure to smooth out any lumps.
- Continue cooking, whisking frequently, until the sauce thickens (about 5 minutes).
- Stir in the Parmesan cheese, nutmeg, salt, and pepper. Remove from heat.

Assemble the Moussaka

- Reduce the oven temperature to 375°F (190°C).
- In a small baking dish (about 6x6 inches), spread a layer of eggplant slices on the bottom.
- Spoon half of the meat sauce over the eggplant.
- Add another layer of eggplant slices and top with the remaining meat sauce.
- Pour the béchamel sauce evenly over the top layer.
- Bake in the preheated oven for 25-30 minutes, until the top is golden brown and bubbly.
- Let it cool for 10 minutes before serving.

Tried & True Tips & Hacks

Eggplant Preparation: To reduce bitterness, sprinkle the eggplant slices with salt and let them sit for 30 minutes before rinsing and patting dry. This step also helps the eggplant slices absorb less oil during roasting.

Béchamel Smoothness: Whisk the béchamel sauce continuously to avoid lumps. If lumps do form, use an immersion blender to smooth out the sauce.

Layering Efficiency: If you have time, prepare the meat sauce and béchamel a day ahead. This allows the flavors to meld together and makes assembly quicker on the day of baking.

Roasting Eggplant: Use parchment paper on your baking sheet to prevent sticking and make clean-up easier.

Leftovers

We made sure that this recipe is perfect for two, so you probably won't end up with any leftovers. But in case you do, or if you double the recipe to make extra, here are some useful ideas:

Freeze Leftovers: Moussaka can be frozen in individual portions. Wrap tightly in plastic wrap or aluminum foil, then place in an airtight container or freezer bag. Reheat in the oven for best results to restore some of the crispiness.

Creative Repurposing: Leftover moussaka can be transformed into a hearty stuffing for bell peppers or zucchini. Simply cut the vegetables in half, scoop out some of the flesh, fill with moussaka, and bake until the vegetables are tender.

Quick Meal: Use leftover moussaka as a base for a Mediterranean casserole. Top with extra béchamel sauce or cheese and bake until heated through and bubbly.

Breakfast Idea: Turn leftover moussaka into a savory breakfast by reheating and serving with a side of scrambled eggs or a fresh green salad.

Cooking Together

Layering Fun: One person can handle slicing and roasting the eggplant while the other prepares the meat sauce and béchamel.

Assembly Line: When assembling, collaborate to layer the ingredients efficiently, ensuring even distribution for a delicious final dish.

DESSERT
Baklava Cups

Baklava might be the ultimate culinary tug-of-war between Turkey and Greece, with both nations proudly claiming it as their own. But I am happily sitting on the fence—I love both countries equally! What I adore even more, though, is making this sweet treat and devouring it all in one go, straight from the oven. Don't judge; I am just living my best life with warm, flaky baklava cups and a generous drizzle of honey syrup.

Ingredients for Two

For the Filling

- 1/2 cup walnuts, finely chopped
- 1/4 cup granulated sugar
- 1/2 teaspoon ground cinnamon
- 1/4 teaspoon ground cloves (optional)

For the Phyllo

- 4 tablespoons unsalted butter, melted
- 6 sheets phyllo dough

For the Honey Syrup

- 1/4 cup honey
- 1 tablespoon water
- 1/4 teaspoon lemon juice

✓ **Prepare Time:**

20 minutes

✓ **CookTime:**

15 minutes

✓ **Total Time:**

35 minutes

✓ **Serving:**

2

Instruction

- Preheat your oven to 350°F (175°C).

For the Filling

- In a small bowl, mix together the chopped walnuts, granulated sugar, ground cinnamon, and ground cloves (if using). Set aside.

For the Cups

- Brush a muffin tin with melted butter to prevent sticking.
- Lay one sheet of phyllo dough on a clean surface and brush with melted butter. Place another sheet on top, and brush with more butter. Repeat until you have layered 3 sheets.
- Cut the stacked phyllo into 4 squares (approximately 4x4 inches each).
- Gently press each square into the muffin tin, creating a cup shape. Repeat with the remaining phyllo sheets.
- Fill each phyllo cup with a tablespoon of the walnut mixture.
- Bake in the preheated oven for 15 minutes, or until the phyllo is golden brown and crispy.

For the Syrup

- While the baklava cups are baking, combine honey, water, and lemon juice in a small saucepan.
- Heat over low heat, stirring occasionally, until the mixture is well combined and slightly thickened. Remove from heat.
- Once the baklava cups are done baking, remove them from the oven and immediately drizzle with the warm honey syrup.
- Allow to cool slightly before serving. Enjoy warm or at room temperature.

Tried & True Tips & Hacks

Crispy Phyllo: For extra crispy phyllo, make sure to brush each sheet generously with melted butter and avoid letting the phyllo sheets dry out.

Nut Alternatives: If you prefer, you can substitute walnuts with other nuts like pistachios or almonds.

Leftovers

Phyllo Dough: Any leftover phyllo dough can be utilized in our Spanakopita recipe from the same chapter or turned into Turkish Sigara Böreği.

Walnut Mixture: If you make extra walnut filling, it can be used as a topping for yogurt or ice cream or even incorporated into other baked goods.

Cooking Together

Phyllo Handling: One person can handle the phyllo dough while the other brushes it with butter and arranges it in the muffin tin. This speeds up the process and ensures even layering.

Mixing Duties: Assign one person to prepare the walnut filling while the other melts the butter and preps the muffin tin. It's a great way to split tasks and keep things moving smoothly.

Filling Fun: Let each person fill the phyllo cups with the walnut mixture. It's a hands-on way to share the cooking process and ensures everyone gets to add their touch.

Syrup Drizzling & Decorating: After baking, take turns drizzling the warm honey syrup over the baklava cups. Then, each person can decorate a baklava cup to make it their own by adding edible flowers, chopped fruit, or chocolate chips. It's a simple task that allows for some creative flair and final touches. Plus, you'll finally get to settle the everlasting argument of who is more artistic in the kitchen once and for all.

DRINK

Ouzo Lemonade for Two

Ouzo is a bit like a love affair—you either can't get enough or you're not quite sure what all the fuss is about. In Greece, many find solace in a small glass of ouzo with ice, enjoyed in a cozy tavern after work, often with a good friend or two. This Ouzo Lemonade recipe is a clever twist that bridges the gap between the lovers and the skeptics. For those who adore ouzo, this cocktail enhances its distinct flavor in a refreshing new way. And for those who might be on the fence, the zesty lemonade and touch of syrup might just be the transformation you need to become an ouzo enthusiast. Cheers to a recipe that makes room for both the passionate and the hesitant— everyone's invited to join the fun!

Ingredients for Two

For the Filling

- 4 oz ouzo
- 4 oz fresh lemon juice (about 2 lemons)
- 2 oz simple syrup (see below for recipe)
- Ice cubes
- 6 oz sparkling water
- Lemon slices and fresh mint for garnish (optional)

For the Simple Syrup

- 1/2 cup granulated sugar
- 1/2 cup water

✓ **Prepare Time:**
20 minutes

✓ **CookTime:**
15 minutes

✓ **Total Time:**
35 minutes

✓ **Serving:**
2

Instruction

For the Simple Syrup

- In a small saucepan, combine granulated sugar and water. Heat over medium heat, stirring occasionally, until the sugar is completely dissolved. Allow to cool before using.

For the Ouzo Lemonade

- In a shaker or mixing glass, combine ouzo, fresh lemon juice, and simple syrup. Stir or shake well to combine.
- Fill two glasses with ice cubes.
- Pour the ouzo mixture evenly over the ice in each glass.
- Top off each glass with sparkling water and stir gently to combine.
- Garnish with lemon slices and fresh mint, if desired.
- Serve immediately and enjoy your refreshing Ouzo Lemonade!

Tried & True Tips & Hacks

Adjust Sweetness: If you prefer a sweeter lemonade, add more simple syrup to taste.

Chill Your Ingredients: For an extra-refreshing drink, chill your ouzo, lemon juice, and sparkling water beforehand.

Garnish Ideas: Experiment with other garnishes, such as cucumber slices or a sprig of rosemary, for a unique twist.

Leftovers

Simple Syrup: Store any leftover simple syrup in a sealed container in the refrigerator for up to a month. It can be used in other cocktails or sweetened beverages.

Half Full Bottle of Ouzo? No worries! Turn it into a cooking ingredient: Ouzo can be used in cooking to add a unique anise flavor to dishes. Try it in sauces, marinades, or even in a glaze for roasted meats. And it gets even better! You can use ouzo as a dessert infusion: Incorporate ouzo into desserts for an adult twist. It works wonderfully in recipes like sorbet or fruit compotes.

Cooking Together

Stir and Sip: One person can mix the ouzo lemonade while the other prepares the garnishes. Enjoy a collaborative moment as you both taste and adjust the sweetness or garnish to perfection.

Personal Touches: Get creative with the garnishes—try adding different fruits or herbs based on your preferences. You can each add your favorite touches, making each glass unique. And with that note, perhaps we reopened the everlasting argument of who is more creative than whom, so if you'll excuse us, we'll hop off to Italy. See you in the next chapter!

CHAPTER 2
ITALY

Romanticizing Life with 'Sprezzatura'

In Italy, there's a word that encapsulates a way of life, a mindset that the Italians have perfected over centuries—sprezzatura. This term, often difficult to translate directly, represents the art of making something complex look effortless. It's about achieving a quiet confidence, a grace under pressure that is both captivating and inspiring. Whether it's the way an Italian navigates a bustling piazza, dresses with impeccable style, or engages in animated conversation, sprezzatura is about mastering the art of nonchalance, where effort is hidden beneath a veneer of simplicity and elegance.

But sprezzatura isn't just about appearances; it's a way of being that suggests a deep inner confidence and an ability to take on challenges with poise. It's not about ignoring the difficulties, but rather embracing them and making the outcome look easy. The Italian way is to approach life with a certain lightness, where even the most complex tasks are executed with an air of effortlessness.

And it's this very concept that I invite you to bring into your kitchen.

When cooking, especially when trying something new or unfamiliar, it's easy to become overwhelmed or to focus too much on getting everything perfect. But Italian cuisine, like Italian life, thrives on the idea that simplicity is key and that sometimes, the most impressive dishes are the ones that are made with ease and confidence. Imagine yourself cooking with the same nonchalance as an Italian, letting your instincts guide you, and using broad, expressive hand gestures to add a touch of theatrical flair (because, why not?).

The beauty of Italian cooking is that it's rooted in simplicity—high-quality ingredients, straightforward techniques, and the belief that food should be a pleasure, not a chore. As you navigate this chapter, I encourage you to channel your inner Italian. Allow the ingredients to speak for themselves, and approach each recipe with the confidence that you can make it look as effortless as a stroll through an Italian countryside.

The magic of sprezzatura in the kitchen is that it allows you to create meals that are elegant and delicious, without the stress or strain that sometimes accompanies cooking. It's about finding joy in the process and knowing that even the simplest dishes can have a profound impact when made with love and care.

So, as you embark on this culinary journey through Italy, remember: you've got this. Let simplicity shine through, trust your instincts, and don't forget to sprinkle a bit of sprezzatura into everything you do. After all, cooking should be as much about enjoying the experience as it is about the final result. And with this mindset, you'll find that even the most elaborate meals can be made with ease, elegance, and a touch of Italian charm.

SALAD

Panzanella with Burrata

Panzanella is the ultimate summer salad, bringing together the humble ingredients of day-old bread and ripe tomatoes in a celebration of simplicity. With creamy burrata added into the mix, this version feels indulgent yet still embodies the effortless elegance of Italian cuisine. Serve this salad with confidence—it's so delicious, no one will guess how easy it was to prepare! If you're looking to add more protein, try including grilled chicken, prosciutto, or even chickpeas for a vegetarian option. Each of these additions complements the flavors without overpowering the dish.

Ingredients For Two

- 2 cups crusty bread, cut into 1-inch cubes (preferably day-old)
- 1 cup cherry tomatoes, halved
- 1/2 cucumber, diced
- 1/4 red onion, thinly sliced
- 1/4 cup fresh basil leaves, torn
- 2 tablespoons extra virgin olive oil
- 1 tablespoon red wine vinegar
- 1/2 teaspoon Dijon mustard
- Salt and freshly ground black pepper, to taste
- 1 burrata cheese ball (about 4 oz)

Prepare Time:

15 Minutes

Cook Time:

10 Minutes

Total Time:

25 Minutes

Serving:

2

Instruction

- Preheat the oven to 350°F (175°C).

- Spread the bread cubes on a baking sheet and bake for about 10 minutes, until they are golden and crisp. Let them cool slightly.

- In a large bowl, combine the toasted bread cubes, cherry tomatoes, cucumber, red onion, and basil leaves.

- In a small bowl, whisk together the olive oil, red wine vinegar, Dijon mustard, salt, and pepper until well combined.

- Drizzle the vinaigrette over the salad and toss gently to coat all the ingredients evenly.

- Divide the salad between two plates. Place half of the burrata on top of each serving.

- Garnish with a little extra basil for the perfect finishing touch.

Tried & True Tips & Hacks

Stale Bread: This salad is a perfect way to use up leftover bread. If your bread isn't stale, just toast it in the oven as directed.

Eco-Friendly Tip: Compost the vegetable scraps to minimize waste and make your cooking more sustainable.
Leftovers

Bread: Any leftover bread cubes can be stored in an airtight container and used as croutons for another salad.

Extra Burrata: Burrata is best enjoyed fresh, but if you have any leftover, store it in its liquid in an airtight container and use it within a day. It's perfect spread on toast or as a creamy topping for pasta.

Repurpose Leftover Salad: If you have leftover Panzanella, it can be refreshed by tossing it with a little extra olive oil and balsamic vinegar. Alternatively, mix it with scrambled eggs for a savory breakfast.

Leftover Protein: If you added grilled chicken or prosciutto and have some left, use it in a sandwich or a wrap the next day.

Cooking Together

Teamwork: One person can handle chopping the vegetables and preparing the bread, while the other whisks together the vinaigrette and arranges the plates.

Customize: Feel free to add other seasonal vegetables or even some olives for an extra burst of flavor.

Bonding Time: Make the most of this time by sharing your favorite part of the day and some thoughts or ideas about how to incorporate more quality time to your daily routine.

APPETIZER

Baked Parmesan Polenta Fries

Polenta is a staple in Italy, enjoyed for breakfast, lunch, or dinner. But did you know that long before it became synonymous with Italian cuisine, corn polenta was being savored by the Aztecs and Mayans? So, shout out to them for laying the groundwork, but I am still claiming polenta as an Italian must-try. Once considered peasant food, polenta is now a star on the menus of five-star restaurants. It's proof that even humble beginnings, when paired with the right confidence and a bit of sprezzatura, can lead to great places. In this case, the great place is Italy.

Ingredients For Two

- 1 (18-oz) tube of pre-cooked polenta
- 2 tablespoons extra virgin olive oil
- 1/4 cup grated Parmesan cheese
- 1/2 teaspoon garlic powder
- 1/2 teaspoon Italian seasoning
- Salt and pepper, to taste
- Marinara sauce, for dipping

Prepare Time:
15 Minutes

Cook Time:
25 Minutes

Total Time:
35 Minutes

Serving:
2

Instruction

- Preheat your oven to 425°F (220°C). Line a baking sheet with parchment paper.

- Slice the pre-cooked polenta into sticks about 1/2 inch thick.

- In a large bowl, toss the polenta sticks with olive oil until evenly coated.

- In a separate small bowl, mix together the Parmesan cheese, garlic powder, Italian seasoning, salt, and pepper.

- Sprinkle the cheese mixture over the polenta sticks, tossing gently to coat.

- Arrange the polenta sticks on the prepared baking sheet in a single layer, making sure they don't touch.

- Bake in the preheated oven for 20-25 minutes, turning once halfway through, until the fries are golden and crispy on the outside.

- Serve immediately with marinara sauce on the side for dipping.

Tried & True Tips & Hacks

Extra Crunch: For an even crispier finish, place the fries under the broiler for the last 1-2 minutes of baking.
Add a Kick: Sprinkle a pinch of red pepper flakes into the cheese mixture for a bit of heat.

Make-Ahead: You can prepare the polenta sticks and coat them with the Parmesan mixture a few hours in advance. Store them in the fridge until you're ready to bake.

Leftovers

Reheat and Revive: Leftover fries can be reheated in the oven at 400°F (200°C) for 5-7 minutes to regain their crispiness.

Polenta Croutons: If you still have leftover fries, cut them into smaller pieces and toss them into a salad as crunchy croutons.

Marinara Sauce: If you just opened a fresh jar of marinara sauce to accompany your polenta fries you are probably left with a hefty amount. But fear not! You can use it in the next recipe, Pasta alla Norma, instead of tomato sauce.

Cooking Together

Divide and Conquer: One person can slice the polenta into sticks while the other prepares the Parmesan coating. This way, you're both involved in the prep work, and it goes twice as fast.

Coating Assembly Line: Create an assembly line where one person tosses the polenta sticks in olive oil, and the other coats them with the Parmesan mixture. This is a fun way to work together and ensures that each fry is perfectly seasoned.

Dipping Duo: While the fries bake, one of you can heat up the marinara sauce and taste-test for seasoning. Once the fries are ready, you can take turns dipping and enjoying them hot out of the oven.

MAIN COURSES
Pasta alla Norma

Don't be fooled by the simple name "Pasta alla Norma" – there's nothing ordinary about this dish! The combination of sautéed eggplant, rich tomato sauce, and creamy ricotta creates a symphony of flavors that's anything but bland. If you happen to have leftover marinara sauce from the polenta fries recipe, don't hesitate to use it here; it's a fantastic way to make the most of your ingredients. While this dish is typically vegetarian, feel free to add a protein of your choice to make it even more satisfying. Dive into this Italian classic, and you'll see that simplicity can be truly extraordinary!

Ingredients For Two

- 6 oz pasta of your choice (penne or rigatoni work well)
- 2 tablespoons extra virgin olive oil, divided
- 1 small eggplant, diced
- 2 cloves garlic, minced
- 1 can (14 oz) crushed tomatoes (or any leftover marinara sauce you have from the Polenta Fries recipe)
- 1/4 teaspoon red pepper flakes (optional)
- Salt and pepper to taste
- 2 oz (about 1/4 cup) ricotta cheese, crumbled
- Fresh basil leaves, torn

Prepare Time:
10 Minutes

Cook Time:
30 Minutes

Total Time:
40 Minutes

Serving:
2

Instruction

- Bring a pot of salted water to a boil. Cook the pasta according to the package instructions until al dente. Drain and set aside.

- While the pasta is cooking, heat 1 tablespoon of olive oil in a large pan over medium heat. Add the diced eggplant and sauté until golden and tender, about 8-10 minutes. Remove from the pan and set aside.

- In the same pan, add the remaining olive oil and minced garlic. Sauté for about 1 minute until fragrant. Pour in the crushed tomatoes (or marinara sauce), red pepper flakes (if using), salt, and pepper. Let the sauce simmer for 10-15 minutes, stirring occasionally.

- Add the sautéed eggplant back into the pan with the tomato sauce. Stir to combine, then toss in the cooked pasta. Mix everything together until the pasta is well coated with the sauce.

- Divide the pasta between two plates. Top with crumbled ricotta and fresh basil leaves. Serve immediately.

Tried & True Tips & Hacks

Meal-Prepping: You can sauté the eggplant ahead of time and store it in the fridge until you're ready to use it.

Pasta Choice: For Pasta alla Norma, a short, sturdy pasta like penne or rigatoni works best. These shapes have enough surface area to hold onto the chunky eggplant and tomato sauce, ensuring every bite is packed with flavor. If you prefer something a bit more delicate, cavatappi or fusilli are also great options for their ability to capture sauce in their twists and turns.

Protein Additions: While this dish is delicious as is, you can add grilled chicken, sausage, or even crisped chickpeas to boost its protein content. If you go for meat, cook it separately and stir it in just before serving to maintain its texture and flavor.

Testing for Al Dente: To check if your pasta is al dente, take a piece and bite into it. It should be tender with a slight firmness in the center. If it's too soft, it's overcooked. Al dente pasta should have a bit of chew and should not be mushy. For the most accurate results, follow the package instructions, but start checking a minute or two before the suggested cooking time ends.

Leftovers

Basil: If you have leftover basil from the Pasta alla Norma, it can be tossed into the Panzanella with Burrata from the beginning of this Italian chapter for added freshness and flavor.

Ricotta: Extra ricotta can be used in the Ricotta and Lemon Cake featured in this chapter, adding a creamy texture and a subtle tang to the dessert.

Eggplants: Any remaining eggplant can be transformed into a delicious Ratatouille in the Southern France chapter, turning your leftovers into a new and flavorful dish.

Cooking Together

Divide and Conquer: Assign different tasks to each person to make the cooking process smoother. One person can handle chopping vegetables while the other focuses on cooking the pasta or preparing the sauce.

Timing is Key: Coordinate cooking times so that everything is ready at the same moment. For instance, start the pasta boiling before you begin sautéing the eggplant to ensure everything finishes simultaneously.

Get Creative: Encourage each person to add their personal touch to the dish. Maybe one person adds extra herbs to the pasta while the other experiments with the seasoning of the sauce.

Set the Scene: Create a fun atmosphere by playing some music and making the cooking process enjoyable. It's a great opportunity to chat and bond while preparing your meal.

Share the Cleanup: Make cleaning up part of the fun. While one person finishes cooking, the other can start tidying up. This way, you both enjoy the meal and the process of preparing it together.

MAIN COURSES

Sheet Pan Chicken Cacciatore

This Sheet Pan Chicken Cacciatore is like a culinary reunion of your favorite ingredients—think tomatoes, olives, and onions, all making a comeback from other recipes in this book. I created this dish for three very good reasons: it tastes fantastic, it simplifies cleanup with just one pan, and it helps use up those leftover ingredients you might have hanging around. Pair it with a glass of the same wine you used in the recipe, and you've got a meal that's both delicious and resourceful. Enjoy the ease and flavor of this hearty, fuss-free feast!

Ingredients For Two

- 1 red bell pepper, sliced
- 1 yellow bell pepper, sliced
- 1 large onion, sliced
- 1 cup cherry tomatoes, halved
- 1/2 cup Kalamata olives, pitted
- 4 bone-in, skin-on chicken thighs
- 3 tablespoons extra virgin olive oil
- Salt and black pepper to taste
- 3 cloves garlic, minced
- 1 tablespoon fresh rosemary, chopped (or 1 teaspoon dried rosemary)
- 1/4 cup white wine

Prepare Time:
10 Minutes

Cook Time:
35- 40 Minutes

Total Time:
50 Minutes

Serving:
2

Instruction

- Preheat your oven to 400°F (200°C).

- Arrange the bell peppers, onion, cherry tomatoes, and olives on a large sheet pan.

- Pat the chicken thighs dry with paper towels. Rub them with olive oil, and season generously with salt and pepper. Place the chicken thighs on the sheet pan with the vegetables.

- Sprinkle the minced garlic and chopped rosemary over the chicken and vegetables.

- Pour the white wine over the chicken and vegetables. This will help to create a flavorful sauce as everything roasts.

- Place the sheet pan in the oven and roast for about 35-40 minutes, or until the chicken reaches an internal temperature of 165°F (74°C) and is golden brown. The vegetables should be tender and slightly caramelized.

- Remove from the oven and let it rest for a few minutes before serving. Enjoy the chicken and vegetables with a side of crusty bread or over a bed of rice or pasta.

Tried & True Tips & Hacks

Wine Pairing: Use the same white wine in your glass as you did in the recipe. This not only complements the flavors of the dish but also makes for a cohesive dining experience.

Leftover Pasta: Serve the Chicken Cacciatore over leftover plain pasta from the Pasta alla Norma recipe. It makes for a hearty, complete meal with minimal extra effort.

Crusty Bread: Enjoy the dish with a side of crusty bread. Any leftover bread can be transformed into Panzanella for a filling salad the next day.

Leftovers

Made Extra? Leftover chicken and vegetables can be used in a hearty soup or mixed into a pasta dish for another easy meal. Simply shred the chicken and mix with some broth or sauce for a quick and tasty dish.

Tomatoes and Olives: Use leftover tomatoes and olives from the Chicken Cacciatore in the Panzanella with Burrata or any of your favorite Mediterranean salads. They add a burst of flavor and texture.

Onions: Leftover onions can be repurposed in the Pasta alla Norma for added sweetness or used in the Ricotta and Lemon Cake for a savory touch. They also work great in the Ratatouille from the French chapter.

Wine: If you have leftover wine from the recipe, it can be enjoyed with other dishes or used in sauces and marinades to add depth of flavor.

Cooking Together

Prep Together: One person can chop the vegetables while the other seasons and prepares the chicken. Working together on prep can make the process faster and more enjoyable.

Mix It Up: Take turns adding ingredients to the sheet pan. This makes it easier to keep track of what's been added and ensures even distribution of flavors.

Taste and Adjust: Before roasting, taste the vegetables and adjust the seasoning if necessary. This way, you can both agree on the flavor profile.

Enjoy the Aromas: As the dish roasts, enjoy the delicious aromas filling your kitchen. Use this time to relax together and set the table.

DESSERT

Ricotta and Lemon Cake

This Ricotta and Lemon Cake is the perfect recipe for beginners, thanks to its straightforward dry-to-wet ingredient method that builds confidence in the kitchen. You'll be amazed at how effortlessly this simple cake transforms into a finger-licking treat that tastes like it came from the most coveted pasticceria in Venice. I used ramekins to make the perfect portions for two, but if you are expecting company, you can triple the recipe and use an 8-inch (20 cm) round cake pan that would serve six. For a casual daily dessert, enjoy it plain and unadorned. If you're feeling a bit more ambitious, elevate it to a 'raffinato' status (as the Italians would say) by decorating it with candied lemon slices and edible flowers for a touch of elegance.

Ingredients For Two

- 1/2 cup (4 oz) well-drained ricotta cheese
- 1/4 cup granulated sugar
- 1 medium egg
- 1/4 cup all-purpose flour
- 1/4 teaspoon baking powder
- A tiny pinch of salt
- 1/4 cup unsalted butter, melted
- Zest of 1 lemon
- 1/2 tablespoon lemon juice
- Powdered sugar for dusting (optional)

Prepare Time:
10 Minutes

Cook Time:
20- 25 Minutes

Total Time:
35 Minutes

Serving:
2

Instruction

- Preheat your oven to 350°F (175°C). Grease two individual ramekins or a small cake pan.

- In a medium bowl, whisk together the ricotta cheese and granulated sugar until smooth and creamy.

- Beat in the egg, mixing well to incorporate into the mixture.

- In a separate bowl, whisk together the flour, baking powder, and a tiny pinch of salt.

- Gradually add the dry ingredients to the wet mixture, mixing until just combined.

- Gently fold in the melted butter, lemon zest, and lemon juice until evenly distributed.

- Pour the batter into the prepared cake pan(s) and smooth the top.

- Bake for 10-15 minutes, or until a toothpick inserted into the center of the cake comes out clean.

- Allow the cake(s) to cool in the pan for 10 minutes before transferring to a wire rack to cool completely.

- Dust with powdered sugar before serving if desired.

Tried & True Tips & Hacks

Make Ahead: This cake can be made ahead of time and stored in an airtight container for up to 3 days.

Enhance Flavor: For extra lemon flavor, you can add a lemon glaze made with powdered sugar and lemon juice.

Texture Tips: Ensure the ricotta cheese is well-drained to avoid excess moisture in the cake batter.

Leftovers

Cake Storing: Store leftover cake in an airtight container at room temperature for up to 3 days or in the refrigerator for up to a week.

Bread Pudding: Cube any leftover cake and use it as the base for a delicious bread pudding. Mix with eggs, milk, sugar, and a bit of vanilla or lemon zest, then bake until golden and set. It's a great way to repurpose leftover cake into a comforting dessert.

French Toast: Transform leftover cake into a unique French toast. Dip slices of the cake into a mixture of beaten eggs and milk, then cook in a skillet until golden on both sides. Serve with fresh fruit, syrup, or a dusting of powdered sugar for a special breakfast treat.

Cooking Together

Measure Together: Have both cooks measure out the ingredients together. This not only makes the process fun but also ensures accuracy. Plus, it's a great way to bond and teach each other about different baking components.

Mix and Whisk: One person can handle mixing the dry ingredients while the other whisks the wet ingredients. When it's time to combine, take turns folding the ingredients together to get a sense of how to achieve the right consistency.

Decorating Fun: When the cake is baked and cooled, have a decorating session together. One person can prepare the toppings, like candied lemon slices or edible flowers, while the other applies them. This turns the final step into a creative activity.

DRINK
Prosecco and Peach Bellini

Prosecco and peaches are the new peaches and cream—a pairing that's simply irresistible. If summer in Italy had a flavor, this would be it. The vibrant, sun-kissed sweetness of ripe peaches blends beautifully with the crisp, bubbly charm of Prosecco, creating a cocktail that's as refreshing as it is "elegante."

Making your own peach purée is incredibly easy and takes this Bellini to another level. Trust me, once you try it, you'll never go back to store-bought versions. Just peel and pit a couple of ripe, juicy peaches and blend them in a food processor. Strain through a fine mesh sieve, and if your peaches aren't as sweet as you'd like, add a touch of sugar or honey to taste. That's it! Your fresh peach purée is now ready to mix with Prosecco for the perfect Bellini.

Ingredients For Two

- 1/2 cup peach purée (fresh or store-bought)
- 1 cup chilled Prosecco
- Ice cubes (optional)
- Peach slices for garnish (optional)

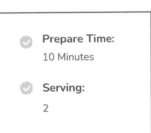

Prepare Time:

10 Minutes

Serving:

2

Instruction

- If using fresh peaches, peel and pit them. Blend the peaches until smooth to make 1/2 cup of peach purée.

- If using store-bought purée, simply measure out 1/2 cup.

- In a mixing glass or small pitcher, combine the peach purée and chilled Prosecco. Stir gently to combine without losing too much of the fizz.

- If desired, add a few ice cubes to two glasses. Pour the peach and Prosecco mixture over the ice.

- Garnish with peach slices if desired.

- Serve immediately while bubbly and refreshing.

Tried & True Tips & Hacks

Chill Prosecco: Make sure the Prosecco is well chilled before mixing to keep the Bellini refreshing.

Adjust Sweetness: If you prefer a sweeter drink, add a touch of simple syrup to the peach purée before mixing.

Flavor Variations: Experiment with other fruit purées, like raspberry or strawberry, for different Bellini flavors.

Leftovers

Peach Purée: If you have leftover peach purée from your Bellinis, consider using it as a topping for yogurt, adding it to smoothies, or mixing it into oatmeal for a fruity kick.

Leftover Peaches: Any extra peaches can be utilized in the Ricotta and Lemon Cake recipe. Add them on top of the cake before baking, or incorporate them into the batter for an extra fruity vibe. Creativity, the Italian way!

Cooking Together

Drink & Play: While preparing the Bellinis, play a game of "Never Have I Ever" with a cooking twist. Each person takes turns making a statement about something they've never done related to food or cooking. For instance, "Never have I ever used a blow torch for cooking." Anyone who has done what's mentioned takes a sip. It's a fun way to learn about each other's culinary experiences and preferences while enjoying your refreshing cocktails.

Thank you for purchasing Louise Mayfield's latest cookbook. To access your bonus travel book as a thank you, please scan the QR code below.

CHAPTER 3
SOUTHERN FRANCE

Nostalgie de la Boue: A Culinary Journey to Simplicity

Ah, Nostalgie de la boue—a phrase that might sound like the title of an avant-garde French film or a chic new cologne, but in reality, it's a poetic concept that translates to "longing for the mud." Imagine Émile Augier, the French poet and dramatist, strolling through the manicured streets of Paris and suddenly yearning for the simple life of a humble mud farmer. It's that peculiar feeling of looking at your polished, high-profile life and suddenly fantasizing about a simpler existence. Perhaps you dream of trading your sleek apartment for a quaint cottage, where the biggest decision of the day is whether to plant roses or tulips.

In essence, Nostalgie de la boue is the romanticized desire to return to a simpler, more authentic way of life, even if it means stepping into the proverbial French mud. It's the charm of the ordinary, the allure of the rustic, and the belief that a simpler life might offer a richer kind of happiness. The idea is not so much about literally going back to the dirt but embracing the simpler pleasures that life can offer, often through the lens of nostalgia.

When it comes to food, I find myself perpetually caught in this nostalgic yearning. There's a part of me that craves simplicity and authenticity in every dish. It's about stripping away the unnecessary, the overly complicated, and the extravagantly pretentious to reveal the pure essence of a recipe.

In this chapter, I've channeled this very sentiment into the heart of French cuisine. I've taken classic French recipes—those elegant dishes that often seem reserved for grand occasions or elaborate gatherings—and distilled them to their core essence. Each recipe is simplified, reimagined to serve just two people, making cooking not only straightforward but also a joyful experience.

Nostalgie de la boue is more than just a longing for the past; it's a celebration of finding joy in simplicity and relishing the authentic flavors of traditional French cooking. By embracing this concept, I hope to take you on a culinary journey where you can enjoy the beauty of classic French dishes, made accessible and practical for two. Revel in the simple pleasure of cooking, savor the flavors of France, and find your happiness in the act of preparing and sharing these beloved recipes.

So, roll up your sleeves, take a deep breath, and let's dive into these nostalgic, simplified French dishes. Because sometimes, the most profound joys are found in the simplest of pleasures, and in this chapter, we'll experience that firsthand.

SALAD

Salade Niçoise Tartines

What's a Tartine, anyway?

Oh la la, the humble tartine—a fancy French term for a slice of bread with toppings that makes you look posh even when you're just lounging in sweatpants. Imagine a sandwich that decided to forgo the second slice of bread, opting instead to strut its stuff with only the top half, proudly showing off its stylish toppings. It's bread's way of saying, "Look at me, I'm special!"

For this recipe, I decided to give the classic French Salade Niçoise a chic makeover by stacking it atop a toasted baguette. The result? A deconstructed masterpiece that's as elegant as it is easy to make. Think of it as a sophisticated open-faced sandwich that might require a fork and knife but guarantees a bit of a chic mess when you're digging in. Because who doesn't enjoy a little refined chaos?

So, grab your sturdy bread and stack it smartly with layers of tuna, eggs, cherry tomatoes, olives, and green beans. Drizzle with a zesty Dijon vinaigrette, and get ready for a meal that's effortlessly classy. And don't worry—if things get a bit messy, remember, that's just part of the tartine charm!

Ingredients For Two

- 2 slices of fresh baguette
- 1/4 cup extra virgin olive oil
- 2 tablespoons Dijon mustard
- 2 tablespoons red wine vinegar
- 1 small clove garlic, minced
- Salt and freshly ground black pepper, to taste
- 1 can (5 oz) of tuna, drained
- 2 hard-boiled eggs, peeled and sliced
- 1/2 cup cherry tomatoes, halved
- 1/4 cup pitted Kalamata olives
- 1/2 cup green beans, trimmed and blanched

Prepare Time:
10 Minutes

Cook Time:
10 Minutes

Total Time:
20 Minutes

Serving:
2

Instruction

- Preheat your oven to 375°F (190°C).

- Place the baguette slices on a baking sheet and toast them in the oven for 5-7 minutes or until golden and crispy. Set aside.

- In a small bowl, whisk together the olive oil, Dijon mustard, red wine vinegar, and minced garlic until well combined.

- Season with salt and freshly ground black pepper to taste. Adjust the seasoning as needed.

- Lay the toasted baguette slices on serving plates. Evenly distribute the drained tuna over each slice.

- Arrange the sliced hard-boiled eggs on top of the tuna.

- Add the cherry tomato halves, Kalamata olives, and blanched green beans on each tartine.

- Spoon or drizzle the prepared Dijon vinaigrette over the assembled tartines.

- Enjoy immediately while the bread is still crispy and the toppings are fresh.

Tried & True Tips & Hacks

Bread Choice: Use a crusty baguette for the best texture, but ciabatta or another rustic bread can be used as a substitute.

Protein Variation: For a variation, you can use grilled chicken or tofu instead of tuna.

Vinaigrette: Adjust the acidity of the vinaigrette with more or less vinegar to suit your taste.

Leftovers

Vinaigrette: Store any leftover vinaigrette in a sealed container in the fridge for up to a week. It can be used on other salads or as a marinade.

Toppings: If you have leftover toppings, they can be used to make a fresh salad or served on crackers for a quick snack.

Bread: Use the leftover baguette to make Goat Cheese and Honey Crostini! You will find a great recipe if you simply flip to the next few pages of this chapter.

Cooking Together

Toast and Chat: While you toast the baguette slices, take the opportunity to chat and catch up. The aroma of toasting bread can make for a cozy, conversational atmosphere.

Vinaigrette Whisk-Off: Have a friendly competition to see who can whisk the vinaigrette the fastest or get the smoothest emulsion. It's a fun way to engage and share some laughs.

Topping Assembly Relay: Divide the toppings and see who can arrange their portion the fastest and most artistically on the baguette slices. You might discover hidden design skills or culinary preferences!

Egg-Slicing Challenge: Slice the hard-boiled eggs together and see who can make the neatest slices. It's a small, engaging task that adds a bit of fun to the preparation.

APPETIZER
Goat Cheese and Honey Crostini

Take your leftover baguette from the Salade Niçoise Tartines and turn it into a magnificent batch of Goat Cheese and Honey Crostini. This way, you can sample two different appetizers as you continue your culinary journey through France. Although crostini is Italian for "toasts," I decided to include this recipe in the French chapter because French cuisine is deeply influenced by its Italian neighbor. I wanted to show you how effortlessly these two rich culinary traditions blend together, creating dishes that are both simple and sophisticated.

Imagine the crispy, golden slices of baguette, topped with creamy goat cheese, drizzled with a touch of honey, and maybe even sprinkled with a few herbs or a crack of black pepper. The sweet and savory combination is a true testament to how basic ingredients can come together to create something utterly delicious.

This Goat Cheese and Honey Crostini is the perfect example of how the essence of French and Italian cuisine can unite in a single bite, offering a harmonious blend of flavors that feels uniquely indulgent and comforting. So, don't let that leftover baguette go to waste—transform it into this elegant appetizer that celebrates the best of both culinary worlds. Bon appétit!

Ingredients For Two

- 4 baguette slices
- Extra virgin olive oil, for brushing
- Salt, to taste
- 2 oz creamy goat cheese
- 1-2 teaspoon honey
- Fresh thyme leaves, for garnish
- Freshly cracked black pepper, to taste

Prepare Time:
5 Minutes

Cook Time:
10 Minutes

Total Time:
15 Minutes

Serving:
2 (Makes 4 crostini)

Instruction

- Preheat your oven to 375°F (190°C).

- Slice the baguette into four ½-inch thick slices. Brush each slice with a light coat of olive oil and season with a pinch of salt.

- Place the baguette slices on a baking sheet.

- Toast in the preheated oven for 8-10 minutes, or until the slices are golden brown and crisp.

- Once toasted, remove the baguette slices from the oven.

- Spread a generous layer of goat cheese on each slice while still warm.

- Drizzle with honey and sprinkle with fresh thyme leaves.

- Add a pinch of freshly cracked black pepper over the top of each crostini for a bit of spice.

- Serve immediately while the crostini are still warm.

Tried & True Tips & Hacks

Perfectly Creamy Goat Cheese: If your goat cheese is too firm to spread, let it sit at room temperature for about 10 minutes before using. You can also mix in a tiny bit of cream or olive oil to make it more spreadable.

Even Toasting: To ensure your baguette slices toast evenly, flip them halfway through the baking time. This helps both sides get that perfect golden crisp.

Honey Drizzle Hack: For a more controlled drizzle, use a spoon to slowly pour the honey in a thin stream, or transfer the honey to a squeeze bottle for easy application.

Extra Flavor Boost: Add a pinch of flaky sea salt on top of the honey for a delicious contrast between the sweet honey and tangy goat cheese.

Advanced Prep: You can toast the baguette slices ahead of time. Just reheat them in the oven for a few minutes before assembling the crostini.

Leftovers

Goat Cheese: If you have leftover goat cheese, don't let it go to waste! You can use it in the Spanish Tortilla with Spinach and Goat Cheese from the Spain chapter. The creamy tanginess of the goat cheese adds a delicious depth to the tortilla.

Honey: That honey jar will come in handy again in this French chapter for making Lavender and Honey Madeleines. The honey adds a lovely floral sweetness that pairs perfectly with the delicate lavender in these classic French treats.

Bread: Leftover baguette slices? Don't throw them out! You can cube them and toast them to make croutons for soups and salads, or even use them to make a savory bread pudding.

Thyme: Fresh thyme is incredibly versatile. Use any leftover thyme to add a fragrant, earthy note to roasted vegetables, or sprinkle it on chicken or fish before baking. You can also dry it and store it for future use or toss it into the next soup or stew you make for an extra burst of flavor.

Cooking Together

Divide and Conquer: One of you can toast the baguette slices while the other preps the toppings. This way, everything comes together quickly, and you both get to play a part in creating this tasty appetizer.

Taste Test Together: Before drizzling the honey on the crostini, taste it together with a bit of goat cheese. Adjust the honey to cheese ratio to suit both your tastes—more honey for a sweeter bite, less for a tangier one.

Garnish as a Duo: One of you can drizzle the honey while the other sprinkles the fresh thyme. Working together like this not only makes the process more fun but also ensures every crostini is perfectly balanced with flavors.

Make it a Contest: See who can make the most beautifully garnished crostini! It's a fun, light-hearted competition that can add a bit of extra enjoyment to your cooking experience.

Enjoy with Wine: Pour a glass of your favorite wine to sip while you cook. It adds a relaxing touch to the experience and pairs perfectly with the goat cheese and honey flavors.

MAIN COURSES
Ratatouille with Poached Eggs

Pronounce in French as "rah-tah-TOO-ee" to sound like a true French even if you are not.

Ratatouille, originally a simple summer stew, emerged from the kitchens of poor Provençal farmers in the 1700s. With hungry bellies to fill and nothing to waste, French peasants would simmer leftover vegetables for hours, creating a hearty, rustic dish. Fast forward to today, and this once-humble stew has found its way into the kitchens of grand chefs in Paris. This dish perfectly captures the essence of Nostalgie de la Boue—a longing for simplicity, for the rich flavors of something born out of necessity, yet celebrated in its purest form.

In this recipe, I've kept that rustic charm intact but added a touch of modernity with poached eggs for extra comfort. If you prefer a vegan option, simply skip the eggs and substitute them with marinated tofu. For those looking to add some protein, consider adding seared chicken, grilled shrimp, or even crispy bacon for a heartier meal. This dish, born out of modest origins, now offers the versatility and elegance to suit any table.

Ingredients For Two

- 1 small eggplant, diced
- 1 small zucchini, diced
- 1 small red bell pepper, diced
- 1 small yellow bell pepper, diced
- 2 medium tomatoes, diced (or 1 can of diced tomatoes)
- 1 small onion, finely chopped
- 2 cloves garlic, minced
- 2 tablespoons extra virgin olive oil
- 1 teaspoon dried thyme (or a few sprigs of fresh thyme to use up any leftovers from the crostini recipe in this chapter)
- Salt and pepper, to taste
- 4 medium eggs
- Fresh basil or parsley, for garnish

Prepare Time:
15 Minutes

Cook Time:
35 Minutes

Total Time:
50 Minutes

Serving:
2

Instruction

- Dice the eggplant, zucchini, bell peppers, and tomatoes. Finely chop the onion and mince the garlic.

- Heat 2 tablespoons of olive oil in a large pan over medium heat. Add the chopped onion and garlic, and sauté until softened and fragrant, about 3-4 minutes.

- Add the diced eggplant, zucchini, and bell peppers to the pan. Cook, stirring occasionally, for 10-12 minutes until the vegetables are tender.

- Stir in the diced tomatoes (or canned tomatoes) and thyme. Season with salt and pepper. Reduce the heat to low and let the mixture simmer for about 15 minutes, allowing the flavors to meld together.

- While the ratatouille is simmering, bring a small pot of water to a gentle simmer. Add a splash of vinegar (optional) to help the eggs hold their shape.

- Crack each egg into a small bowl, then gently slide them one at a time into the simmering water. Cook for 3-4 minutes for a runny yolk or longer if you prefer a firmer yolk.

- Use a slotted spoon to carefully remove the poached eggs and set them aside.

- Once the ratatouille is ready, divide it evenly between two plates or shallow bowls.

- Top each serving with two poached eggs.

- Garnish with fresh basil or parsley. Serve warm, with crusty bread on the side if desired.

Tried & True Tips & Hacks

Vegetable Prep: Dice the vegetables into even-sized pieces so they cook uniformly.

Poaching Eggs: For perfectly poached eggs, keep the water at a gentle simmer, not a rolling boil. Use fresh eggs for the best results.

Bread Pairing: Serve with crusty bread to soak up the delicious juices, or use the leftover bread to make crostini, topped with goat cheese and honey from another recipe in this chapter.

Leftover Ratatouille: Leftover ratatouille can be used as a topping for pizza, tossed with pasta, or served with grilled chicken or fish.

Leftovers

Next-Day Breakfast: Reheat the leftover Ratatouille and serve it over toast with a fried egg on top for a quick and flavorful breakfast.

Pasta Sauce: Use the leftover vegetables as a rich, flavorful sauce for pasta. Just toss it with cooked pasta and sprinkle some grated cheese on top.

Sandwich Filler: Stuff the leftover Ratatouille into a baguette with some goat cheese for a hearty and delicious sandwich.

Pizza Topping: Spread the leftovers over a pizza crust, top with cheese, and bake for a rustic, vegetable-packed pizza.

Protein-Packed Meal: Pair the leftovers with grilled chicken, fish, or sausage for a simple yet satisfying dinner.

Cooking Together

Teamwork: One person can handle the vegetable chopping while the other sautés them, making the process quicker and more interactive.

Poaching Eggs Together: If you're both new to poaching eggs, take turns trying it out. It's a fun skill to master together.

Creative Garnishing: One of you can poach the eggs while the other focuses on garnishing the dish. Fresh herbs and a sprinkle of cheese can elevate the presentation.

Taste Test: Before serving, taste the ratatouille together to check the seasoning. Adjust with salt, pepper, or a splash of olive oil as needed.

MAIN COURSES
Chicken Provençal

Chicken Provençal is what happens when France borders Italy. A true embodiment of Mediterranean magic, where the flavors of France seamlessly mingle with Italian influences.

This dish is a testament to how simple ingredients, when combined with a touch of culinary finesse, can create something truly extraordinary. Imagine the rustic charm of Provence meeting the vibrant essence of Italian cuisine, resulting in a dish that bursts with flavor and sophistication.

I find chicken thighs to be often underestimated and overlooked. But the reality is that not only are they more affordable than other cuts, but they're also incredibly versatile and easy to find at any grocery store. Their rich, succulent texture is perfect for absorbing the robust flavors of a Provençal sauce, making them a standout choice for this dish. Once you master the art of cooking chicken thighs, you'll find yourself seeing them in a whole new light—an ingredient that's as delicious as it is budget-friendly.

In Provençal French cooking, the magic lies in transforming humble, everyday ingredients into something special. This recipe captures that essence beautifully. It's a delicious reminder that the best meals often come from the simplest ingredients, enhanced by the artistry of Provençal cooking.

I suggest doubling the recipe and jumping to the 'leftovers' section. You'll be amazed at the possibilities and potential! From soups to salads or pasta and sandwiches, there are so many ideas to make the most of this dish!

Ingredients For Two

- 2 bone-in, skin-on chicken thighs
- 1 tablespoon extra virgin olive oil
- 1/2 small onion, finely chopped
- 2 cloves garlic, minced
- 1/4 cup white wine (optional)
- 1/2 cup cherry tomatoes, halved
- 1/4 cup pitted green or black olives, halved
- 1/2 cup chicken broth
- 1/2 teaspoon dried thyme
- 1/2 teaspoon dried rosemary
- 1/4 teaspoon red pepper flakes (optional)
- Salt and black pepper to taste
- Fresh parsley, chopped (for garnish)
- Crusty bread for serving

Prepare Time:
15 Minutes

Cook Time:
35 Minutes

Total Time:
50 Minutes

Serving:
2

Instruction

- Pat the chicken thighs dry with paper towels and season generously with salt and black pepper on both sides.

- Heat the olive oil in a large skillet over medium-high heat.

- Add the chicken thighs, skin-side down, and cook for 5-7 minutes, or until the skin is golden and crispy.

- Flip the chicken thighs and cook for another 3-4 minutes on the other side. Remove the chicken from the skillet and set aside.

- In the same skillet, add the chopped onion and garlic. Sauté for 2-3 minutes until softened and fragrant.

- If using, add the white wine to the skillet, scraping up any browned bits from the bottom of the pan. Let it simmer for 2 minutes to reduce slightly.

- Add the cherry tomatoes, olives, chicken broth, thyme, rosemary, and red pepper flakes (if using) to the skillet. Stir to combine.

- Return the chicken thighs to the skillet, skin-side up, nestling them into the sauce.

- Reduce the heat to medium-low, cover the skillet, and let the chicken simmer for 20-25 minutes, or until the chicken is cooked through (internal temperature of 165°F or 74°C) and the sauce has thickened slightly.

- Taste the sauce and adjust seasoning with salt and pepper if needed.

- Garnish with freshly chopped parsley.

- Serve the chicken with a generous ladle of the sauce and crusty bread on the side to soak up the delicious juices.

Tried & True Tips & Hacks

Perfectly Crispy Skin

Dry the Chicken. Ensure the chicken thighs are thoroughly dried with paper towels before cooking. This helps achieve a crispy, golden-brown skin.

Preheat the Skillet. Make sure your skillet is hot before adding the chicken. This promotes a nice sear and helps the skin crisp up.

Enhance the Flavor

Marinate Ahead. For an extra boost of flavor, marinate the chicken thighs in olive oil, garlic, and herbs for a few hours or overnight. This infuses the meat with additional depth.

Use Fresh Herbs. While dried herbs are great, using fresh thyme and rosemary, if available, will add a brighter, more vibrant flavor to the dish.

Make the Sauce Richer

Deglaze with Wine. If you're using white wine, let it simmer until it reduces by half to concentrate the flavors. If you prefer not to use wine, a splash of lemon juice or a bit of balsamic vinegar can add acidity and balance.

Add a Touch of Sweetness. A pinch of sugar or a splash of honey can help balance the acidity of the tomatoes and enhance the overall flavor of the sauce.

Cooking Tips

Simmer Gently. Keep the heat at a gentle simmer to ensure the chicken cooks evenly and the sauce doesn't reduce too quickly.

Use a Lid. Covering the skillet while simmering helps the chicken stay moist and allows the flavors to meld better.

Leftovers

Chicken Provençal Pasta: Shred any leftover chicken and toss it with cooked pasta and some of the sauce. Top with fresh herbs and grated Parmesan cheese for a quick and satisfying meal.

Chicken Provençal Salad: Use the leftover chicken and sauce as a flavorful topping for a salad. Add mixed greens, olives, and some crumbled feta or goat cheese for a Mediterranean-inspired salad.

Chicken Provençal Sandwich: Shred the chicken and place it on a crusty baguette or ciabatta roll. Add some fresh greens and a spread of Dijon mustard or aioli for a delicious sandwich.

Chicken Provençal Soup: Combine the leftover chicken and sauce with additional chicken broth and some vegetables like carrots or potatoes to make a hearty soup.

Cooking Together

Encourage Each Other: Cooking together should be a fun experience, so encourage and support each other throughout the process.

Enjoy Together: Sit down and enjoy the meal you've created together. Share your thoughts on the dish and savor the fruits of your teamwork.

Reflect: After the meal, reflect on what went well and what you might do differently next time. It's a great way to improve your cooking skills and make future experiences even better.

DESSERT
Lavender and Honey Madeleines

In the Ricotta and Lemon Cake recipe, I discussed the wet-to-dry ingredients method and how mastering it can build your confidence in baking. When it comes to madeleines, there are various recipes and techniques out there, but after many tests and careful consideration, this is the one that made the cut for the book.

This particular recipe stands out for several reasons. Firstly, it's incredibly easy to make and yields just 6 madeleines, which is perfect for 2 people. You can savor 2 each as a fantastic and light dessert and save a couple to dunk in your coffee the next morning. But to be honest, I never managed to save any—these little treats are so irresistible that I ended up eating them all in one sitting!

Another reason this recipe was chosen is its undeniable French charm. There's a certain "je ne sais quoi" about these madeleines—a term that translates to "I don't know what" in French. It captures that elusive, indescribable quality that makes these sponge cakes uniquely sophisticated and delicious. They embody a classic French elegance that's both comforting and refined, making them the perfect addition to any dessert repertoire.

Ingredients For Two

- 1/4 cup (1/2 stick) unsalted butter, plus extra for greasing
- 1/4 cup all-purpose flour
- 1/8 teaspoon baking powder
- 1/4 cup granulated sugar
- 1 medium egg
- 2 tablespoons honey
- 1/2 teaspoon dried culinary lavender (finely crushed)
- Powdered sugar (optional, for dusting)

Prepare Time:
15 Minutes

Cook Time:
8-10 Minutes

Total Time:
30 Minutes

Serving:
2

Instruction

- Preheat your oven to 375°F (190°C).

- Grease a madeleine pan with butter and lightly flour it, or use a non-stick spray.

- Melt the butter in a small saucepan over low heat. Let it cool slightly.

- In a small bowl, sift together the flour and baking powder. Set aside.

- In a medium bowl, whisk the sugar and egg together until light and frothy (about 2 minutes).

- Add the honey and mix until combined.

- Gradually whisk in the melted butter until the mixture is smooth.

- Gently fold the flour mixture into the wet ingredients until just combined. Be careful not to overmix.

- Fold in the finely crushed lavender.

- Spoon the batter into the prepared madeleine pan, filling each mold about 3/4 full.

- Bake in the preheated oven for 8-10 minutes, or until the edges are golden brown and the centers spring back when lightly touched.

- Remove the madeleines from the oven and let them cool in the pan for about 5 minutes. Gently remove them from the pan and transfer to a wire rack to cool completely.

- If desired, dust with powdered sugar before serving.

Tried & True Tips & Hacks

Clarify Butter: For an extra touch of sophistication and to prevent browning, use clarified butter. Simply melt the butter, let it cool slightly, and then skim off any milk solids that rise to the top.

Chill the Pan: After greasing and flouring the madeleine pan, chill it in the refrigerator for 10-15 minutes. This helps the madeleines develop their signature hump as they bake.

Whisk Egg and Sugar Well: Ensure that the egg and sugar mixture is whisked until light and frothy. This step incorporates air, helping the madeleines achieve a light, airy texture.

Fold, Don't Stir: When incorporating the flour into the wet ingredients, fold gently rather than stirring vigorously. This preserves the air bubbles and helps maintain a light texture.

Preheat Properly: Make sure your oven is fully preheated before baking. A hot oven helps the madeleines rise quickly and develop their characteristic bump.

Don't Overbake: Keep a close eye on the madeleines during the last few minutes of baking. They should be golden around the edges and spring back when touched. Overbaking can make them dry.

Cool in the Pan: Allow the madeleines to cool in the pan for about 5 minutes before transferring them to a wire rack. This helps them retain their shape and makes them easier to remove.

Invert Pan: Gently tap the pan on the counter to help release the madeleines if they don't come out easily. You can also use a small knife to loosen the edges if needed.

Leftovers

Madeleine Crumbs as Topping: If any madeleines become overly dry, crumble them up to use as a topping for yogurt, ice cream, or fruit salads.

Dessert Trifle: Use leftover madeleines in a dessert trifle. Layer crumbled madeleines with fruit, custard, and whipped cream for a delicious and elegant dessert.

Pair with Beverages: Leftover madeleines make excellent dunkers for your coffee or tea. Their subtle flavors are perfect for a quick and satisfying snack.

Cooking Together

Set Up the Workspace: Use this recipe as an excuse to work on your organizing skills together. Organize Tools —mixing bowls, measuring cups and spoons, a whisk, a sifter, and the madeleine pan. Ensure the workspace is clean and accessible.

Clear the Counter: Keep the counter uncluttered to allow space for mixing, pouring, and decorating.

DRINK
Kir Royale

I have a confession to make: I prefer old-school champagne glasses over flutes, and I firmly believe that Kir Royale tastes even better in those classic glasses. There's something wonderfully nostalgic about sipping this elegant cocktail from a broad, vintage glass that just seems to enhance the experience. However, I'll leave the choice of glass to you. My focus remains on providing the perfect recipe for your French escape. So, whether you choose flutes or classic champagne glasses, you can be assured that this Kir Royale recipe will deliver the sophisticated taste and charm you're looking for. Cheers to your French-inspired adventure!

Ingredients For Two

- 1 oz crème de cassis (blackcurrant liqueur)
- 4 oz chilled champagne or sparkling wine
- Lemon twist or fresh blackcurrants (for garnish, optional)

Instruction

✓ **Prepare Time:**
5 Minutes

✓ **Serving:**
2

- Prepare the Glasses: Chill your champagne glasses in the refrigerator or freezer for a few minutes before serving. This helps keep the cocktail cold and refreshing.

- Add 1/2 oz (15 ml) of crème de cassis to each chilled champagne flute. Carefully pour the chilled champagne or sparkling wine into each glass, filling it to the top. Pour slowly to avoid excessive foam and to maintain the bubbles.

- If desired, garnish with a lemon twist or a few fresh blackcurrants for an extra touch of elegance.

- Serve the Kir Royale immediately while it's still bubbly and chilled.

Tried & True Tips & Hacks

Use High-Quality Ingredients: Choose a good-quality champagne or sparkling wine and crème de cassis for the best flavor. A brut or extra brut champagne works well, as it balances the sweetness of the crème de cassis.

Serve Chilled: Ensure both the champagne and the crème de cassis are well-chilled before preparation for the best experience.

Pour Gently: When adding the champagne, pour gently over the back of a spoon or down the side of the glass to minimize foam and preserve the bubbles.

Leftovers

Crème de Cassis: Keep It Sealed: Store any leftover crème de cassis in its original bottle, tightly sealed to maintain its flavor and prevent evaporation. Crème de cassis has a long shelf life due to its high sugar and alcohol content. It can typically last for several years if stored properly.

Use leftover crème de cassis in other cocktails, such as a classic Kir (with white wine), or as a flavoring in desserts like sorbets or sauces.

Incorporate it into mixed drinks or spritzers for a fruity twist.

Champagne or Sparkling Wine: Reseal and Refrigerate: If you have leftover champagne or sparkling wine, re-cork it using a champagne stopper or a well-sealed plastic wrap and store it in the refrigerator. This helps maintain its fizz and freshness. Consider using a champagne stopper, which creates a tight seal to preserve the bubbles.

Cocktails and Mimosas: Use the leftover sparkling wine in other cocktails or mimosas. It's perfect for adding a touch of effervescence to a variety of drinks.

Cooking: Sparkling wine can be used in cooking, such as in sauces or risottos, to add a subtle complexity to your dishes.

Cooking Together

Relax and Enjoy: After preparing the drinks, take the time to relax and enjoy your creation. Share your thoughts on the taste and experience.

Plan Future Cocktails: If you enjoyed making Kir Royale together, consider planning future cocktails or recipes to try out as a team.

CHAPTER 4
SPAIN

Spain is a country where the rhythm of life is set to its own unique beat, and one of the most fascinating aspects of Spanish culture is their late mealtimes.

Take a look at a map, and you'll notice that Spain sits along the same longitude as the UK, Portugal, and Morocco, meaning it should naturally be in Greenwich Mean Time. However, Spain operates on Central European Time, aligning it with cities like Belgrade, more than 2,500 kilometers east of Madrid.

This time zone anomaly has had a lasting impact on the daily lives of Spaniards. To cope with the late nights and delayed schedules, they've adapted with some well-established traditions. A typical Spanish day includes a mid-morning coffee break known as "el desayuno" and a leisurely two-hour lunch break in the afternoon. This longer midday break not only allows for a substantial meal but also provides the perfect opportunity to enjoy one of Spain's most cherished traditions: the siesta. This afternoon nap is more than just a luxury; it's a necessity for many Spaniards, helping them recharge for the evening ahead, which often stretches late into the night.

To truly embrace the Spanish way of life, I suggest planning an entire day around the recipes from this chapter. Start with a traditional breakfast, enjoy a slow and hearty lunch, indulge in a siesta, and then savor a late dinner—Spanish style. I'll give you the recipes; the rest is up to you.

Spain's culinary landscape is as diverse as its culture, and there's an old Spanish proverb that encapsulates this diversity: "In the north, you stew; in the center, you roast; and in the south, you fry." While this saying is a simplification, it does reflect the distinct regional differences in Spanish cuisine. In the northern regions, hearty stews like "fabada" and "cocido" are common, while the central areas favor roasted meats such as "cochinillo" (suckling pig). Down south, in the warmer climates of Andalusia, frying is an art form, with dishes like "pescaíto frito" (fried fish) being a staple.

As you explore the recipes in this chapter, you'll get a taste of these regional specialties and experience the rich culinary traditions that make Spain such a vibrant gastronomic destination, but in a simple, easy-to-follow format. From orange and olive salads to paella, each dish tells a story of the country's history, culture, and the unique rhythm of life that makes Spain so enchanting. So, prepare to dine late, indulge in a siesta, and let the flavors of Spain take you on a delicious journey through its diverse regions.

SALAD

Orange and Olive Salad with Smoked Paprika Vinaigrette

If you have 10 minutes, I have the perfect salad for you two. I'll be honest—I'm not usually one to enjoy fruit in a salad, but this recipe is a testament to how amazing this combination can be. The sweetness of the oranges is perfectly balanced by the saltiness of the Kalamata olives, creating a harmony of flavors that completely changed my mind.

The real game-changer here is the smoked paprika vinaigrette. It adds a smoky depth that ties everything together beautifully. I love making a big batch of this vinaigrette every Sunday and keeping it in the fridge to dress my salads throughout the week. It's a simple trick that makes eating my greens something I actually look forward to—and believe me, I don't complain too much! This salad is refreshing, vibrant, and the perfect way to start any meal.

Ingredients For Two

For the Salad

- 2 large oranges
- 1/4 small red onion, thinly sliced
- 1/3 cup Kalamata olives, pitted and halved
- 2 tablespoons fresh parsley, chopped

For the Smoked Paprika Vinaigrette

- 2 tablespoons extra virgin olive oil
- 1 tablespoon red wine vinegar
- 1/2 teaspoon smoked paprika
- 1/2 teaspoon honey (optional, for a touch of sweetness)
- Salt and pepper to taste

	Prepare Time:
	10 Minutes
	Serving:
	2

Instructions

- Peel the oranges, removing as much of the white pith as possible. Slice them into 1/4-inch thick rounds and arrange them on a serving plate.

- Scatter the thinly sliced red onion and halved Kalamata olives over the orange slices.

- Sprinkle with freshly chopped parsley.

- In a small bowl, whisk together the olive oil, red wine vinegar, smoked paprika, and honey (if using). Season with salt and pepper to taste.

- Whisk until the dressing is well combined and slightly thickened.

- Drizzle the smoked paprika vinaigrette over the orange and olive salad, ensuring an even coating.

- Serve the salad immediately, allowing the flavors to meld and the vinaigrette to enhance the sweetness of the oranges and the briny olives.

Tried & True Tips & Hacks

Supreme the Oranges: For a cleaner presentation, try supreming the oranges. This means cutting away the peel and pith, then slicing between the membranes to release perfect segments of orange. It looks elegant and ensures there's no bitterness from the pith.

Chill Before Serving: For an extra-refreshing salad, chill the orange slices and olives in the fridge before assembling the salad. This also helps the flavors meld together better.

Make the Vinaigrette in Bulk: Double or triple the vinaigrette recipe and store it in a sealed jar in the fridge. This way, you have a delicious dressing ready to go for any salad during the week. Just give it a good shake before using.

Olive Variety: While Kalamata olives are delicious, feel free to experiment with other types of olives like Castelvetrano or even a mixed olive medley. Each brings a slightly different flavor profile to the dish.

Enhance the Flavor: For a more robust flavor, consider adding a pinch of crushed red pepper flakes to the vinaigrette for a little heat or a splash of orange juice for extra citrusy brightness.

Enhance the Flavor: For a more robust flavor, consider adding a pinch of crushed red pepper flakes to the vinaigrette for a little heat or a splash of orange juice for extra citrusy brightness.

Add Texture: If you like a bit of crunch, try adding some toasted almonds, pine nuts, or even a handful of crisped chickpeas on top of the salad.

Boost with Protein: To make this salad a more filling and complete meal, add a protein like grilled chicken, shrimp, or even thinly sliced prosciutto. Simply prepare your protein of choice and layer it on top of the salad. The smoky vinaigrette pairs wonderfully with these proteins, enhancing the overall flavor and turning this light starter into a satisfying dish.

Leftovers

Kalamata Olives: Any leftover Kalamata olives can be stored in an airtight container in the refrigerator and used in a variety of dishes. They're perfect for adding a briny, savory kick to salads, pasta, or even as a snack. If you're planning to explore the French chapter, you can use these olives in the Salade Niçoise Tartines recipe, where they'll add a deliciously authentic touch.

Oranges: Leftover oranges can be enjoyed as a refreshing snack on their own, added to a fruit salad, or squeezed for fresh orange juice. You can also use orange slices to brighten up other salads or incorporate them into desserts like a citrus sorbet or cake. And my favorite idea (hopefully now yours, too) is to make a delicious Ricotta and Orange Cake by following the Ricotta and Lemon Cake recipe from the chapter of Italy and swapping lemons for oranges! How cool is that?

Smoked Paprika Vinaigrette: Any extra vinaigrette can be stored in a sealed jar in the fridge for up to a week. Use it to dress other salads, drizzle over roasted vegetables, or even as a marinade for chicken or fish. The smoky, tangy flavor adds a delicious twist to many dishes.

Red Onion: If you have leftover red onion, thinly slice it and store it in the fridge. It's a great addition to sandwiches, burgers, or other salads. You can also pickle the slices in vinegar and sugar for a tangy, crunchy topping that lasts longer.

Cooking Together

Discuss the Recipe: Before starting, go over the recipe together and assign tasks based on each person's strengths and preferences. This ensures that everything runs smoothly and makes the cooking process more enjoyable.

Prep Ingredients: Have all ingredients prepped and measured before you begin. This includes slicing the oranges, halving the olives, and making the vinaigrette. Prepping together can also be a fun part of the cooking experience.

Assign Tasks: One person can focus on assembling the salad while the other prepares the vinaigrette. This division of labor keeps things efficient and allows both of you to stay engaged and productive.

Coordinate Timing: Make sure to coordinate timing, especially if you're adding any protein or extra elements to the salad. This way, everything is ready to serve at the same time.

Communicate: Keep communication open to avoid stepping on each other's toes. Share your progress and check in frequently to ensure you're both on the same page.

APPETIZER

Garlic Shrimp (Gambas al Ajillo)

This Garlic Shrimp (Gambas al Ajillo) is truly one of my favorite recipes from the book and holds a special place in my heart. It epitomizes versatility and delicious simplicity, proving that gourmet cooking doesn't have to be complicated to make you feel like you're dining at a five-star restaurant in Spain. The combination of succulent shrimp sautéed in fragrant garlic and smoky red pepper flakes finished with a splash of lemon juice is not just an appetizer—it's an experience.

This dish embodies the spirit of Spanish tapas: bold, flavorful, and, believe me, truly uncomplicated. It's the perfect example of how a few well-chosen ingredients can create a meal that's both elegant and effortless. What I love most about this recipe is how easily it transitions from a starter to a star player in a variety of other dishes.

To celebrate the versatility of this dish, I've dedicated a whole section to exploring what you can do with the leftovers besides simply serving them as an appetizer. Whether you're transforming it into a hearty shrimp and grits dish, tossing it with pasta for a quick weeknight meal, or incorporating it into a zesty shrimp taco, the possibilities are endless. This section aims to inspire you to see Garlic Shrimp in a new light, showcasing how this simple yet spectacular dish can elevate your everyday meals with just a bit of creativity.

So, enjoy this recipe as a fantastic start to your meal, but don't stop there. Embrace its adaptability and let it inspire you to experiment with new flavors and dishes. With Garlic Shrimp, you have a gateway to a culinary adventure that brings the essence of Spanish dining right into your kitchen.

Ingredients For Two

For the Shrimp

- 1/2 lb large shrimp, peeled and deveined
- Salt and black pepper, to taste
- 3 tablespoons extra virgin olive oil
- 4 cloves garlic, thinly sliced
- 1/4 teaspoon red pepper flakes (adjust to taste)
- 1 tablespoon fresh lemon juice
- 1 tablespoon fresh parsley, chopped (for garnish)

For Serving

- Crusty bread, sliced (such as baguette or ciabatta)

Prepare Time:
10 Minutes

Cook Time:
10 Minutes

Total Time:
20 Minutes

Serving:
2

Instructions

- Pat the shrimp dry with paper towels. Season lightly with salt and black pepper.

- In a medium skillet, heat the olive oil over medium heat until shimmering.

- Add the sliced garlic to the skillet. Sauté for about 1-2 minutes, stirring frequently, until the garlic is golden and fragrant but not burnt.

- Add the red pepper flakes and cook for an additional 30 seconds to release their flavor.

- Add the shrimp to the skillet in a single layer. Cook for about 2-3 minutes per side, or until the shrimp turn pink and opaque. Be careful not to overcook the shrimp, as they can become tough.

- Once the shrimp are cooked through, remove the skillet from heat. Drizzle the lemon juice over the shrimp and give it a final stir.

- Transfer the garlic shrimp to a serving dish and garnish with freshly chopped parsley.

- Serve immediately with slices of crusty bread for dipping into the flavorful oil.

Tried & True Tips & Hacks

Perfect Garlic: Slice the garlic thinly and sauté it over medium heat to prevent burning. Burnt garlic can turn bitter, so watch it closely and remove it from heat as soon as it turns golden brown.

Shrimp Size: Use large shrimp for this recipe, as they cook quickly and stay juicy. Make sure the shrimp are all roughly the same size to ensure even cooking.

Prepping Shrimp: To save time, buy pre-peeled and deveined shrimp. If you're peeling them yourself, keep a bowl of water handy to rinse your hands and prevent the shrimp from sticking.

Oil Temperature: Ensure the olive oil is hot before adding the garlic. It should shimmer but not smoke. This ensures the garlic infuses the oil effectively without burning.

Taste and Adjust: Before serving, taste the shrimp and adjust seasoning if needed. A touch more salt, a dash of additional lemon juice, or an extra sprinkle of red pepper flakes can make a big difference.

Bread Serving: Lightly toast the crusty bread if you prefer it crispy. This adds a delightful crunch and makes it even better for soaking up the flavorful garlic oil.

Herb Variations: Fresh parsley is a classic garnish, but you can also use cilantro or chives for a different twist. Adding a bit of lemon zest on top can enhance the citrusy flavor.

Leftovers

Leftover Oil: The garlic-infused olive oil leftover from cooking the shrimp is full of flavor. Store it in an airtight container in the fridge and use it for cooking or as a dipping oil for bread.

Leftover Garlic Shrimp In the hopes of highlighting how versatile this recipe is, I would like to dedicate some space to the many wonderful things you can do with any (if any) leftovers. So follow along and bet you'll want to make extra whenever you make this recipe.

Shrimp and Grits: Serve the garlic shrimp over creamy grits for a comforting Southern-inspired meal. The shrimp's flavorful oil pairs beautifully with the richness of the grits.

Shrimp Fried Rice: Stir-fry the garlic shrimp with cooked rice, vegetables (like peas, carrots, and bell peppers), and a splash of soy sauce. Garnish with green onions for added freshness.

Shrimp Quesadillas: Chop the shrimp and place it between tortillas with cheese and any additional fillings like sautéed peppers or onions. Cook in a skillet until the tortillas are crispy and the cheese is melted.

Shrimp Pasta: Toss the leftover shrimp with pasta, such as spaghetti or linguine, and a splash of the garlic-infused oil. Add a bit of lemon zest or fresh herbs for a fresh finish.

Shrimp Sandwiches: Use the shrimp to make a tasty sandwich. Place the shrimp on a toasted bun with lettuce, tomato, and a drizzle of aioli or mayonnaise.

Shrimp and Avocado Salad: Toss chopped shrimp with mixed greens, cherry tomatoes, avocado slices, and a simple vinaigrette. Add some crumbled feta or goat cheese for extra flavor.

Shrimp Tacos: Use the shrimp as a filling for tacos. Add shredded cabbage, avocado slices, and a squeeze of lime. Top with a creamy sauce or salsa for added flavor.

Shrimp Frittata: Incorporate the shrimp into a frittata with eggs, cheese, and vegetables. Bake until set and golden for a savory brunch or light dinner.

Shrimp Soup: Add the shrimp to a broth-based soup. A light tomato or vegetable broth with some added greens and noodles makes a flavorful and satisfying soup.

Shrimp Stuffed Bell Peppers: Mix chopped shrimp with cooked rice or quinoa and some diced vegetables. Stuff the mixture into halved bell peppers and bake until the peppers are tender.

Cooking Together

Plan the Process: Before starting, review the recipe together and assign tasks based on each person's strengths or preferences. For example, one person can handle peeling and deveining the shrimp while the other prepares the garlic and sets up the skillet.

Prep Ingredients Together: Work side by side to slice the garlic, measure out the olive oil, and prepare the red pepper flakes. This teamwork makes prep work faster and more enjoyable, and it ensures all ingredients are ready when you start cooking.

Coordinate Timing: While one person heats the olive oil, the other can prepare the garlic and red pepper flakes. Make sure to keep an eye on the garlic to avoid burning, and communicate about when to add the shrimp to the skillet.

Seasoning Together: Once the shrimp are cooked, taste them and adjust the seasoning as needed. This is a great opportunity to discuss flavors and preferences and to decide if more lemon juice or seasoning is needed.

Share the Experience: Use this time to chat, laugh, and enjoy each other's company. Cooking together is as much about the experience as it is about the final dish, so embrace the fun of preparing a meal with someone you care about.

Be Creative: Don't be afraid to experiment with variations of the recipe together. Maybe try adding a new herb or spice or adjust the amount of red pepper flakes for different levels of heat. Cooking together is a great opportunity to be creative and discover new flavors.

Clean Up as a Team: After enjoying your meal, tackle the cleanup together. One person can wash the dishes while the other wipes down the counters and puts away leftovers. Sharing this task makes it less of a chore and more of a shared effort.

MAIN COURSES

Paella for Two

In the world of Spanish cuisine, few dishes capture the essence of traditional cooking quite like paella. Among its many revered elements, one stands out as both a mark of culinary skill and a delicious reward: the socarrat. This crispy, golden layer of rice that forms at the bottom of the pan is the pinnacle of paella perfection, and it's one of the reasons I'm excited to share this recipe with you.

The art of achieving socarrat is not just about technique; it's about understanding the soul of paella. This distinct layer is created when the rice is cooked over a low flame until it develops a crispy, caramelized crust. It's a delicate balance of timing and temperature, and mastering it elevates a good paella to something truly extraordinary. The socarrat adds a very special crunch and deepens the flavor of the dish, embodying the heart of Spanish culinary tradition.

In a sea of paella recipes, this one stands out not only for its rich, aromatic flavors but also for its manageability. This recipe is designed for two, making it a perfect choice for an intimate meal while still delivering the authentic experience of Spanish cooking. With tender chicken, smoky chorizo, and saffron-infused rice, this paella captures the essence of Spain in a portion that's both practical and indulgent.

So, after much consideration, I've included this recipe in the book because it embodies the true spirit of paella, offering a taste of the art of socarrat without overwhelming the home cook. It's a celebration of flavor and tradition, crafted to be approachable yet impressive. Whether you're a paella aficionado or a curious beginner, this dish provides a genuine taste of Spain, making it easier to appreciate and achieve the crispy, delectable socarrat that defines great paella. Enjoy this recipe and savor the satisfaction of creating a dish that embodies the best of Spanish culinary artistry.

Ingredients For Two

- 1 tablespoon extra virgin olive oil
- 1/2 lb chicken thighs, boneless and skinless, cut into bite-sized pieces
- 1/4 lb chorizo sausage, sliced
- 1 small onion, finely chopped
- 1 red bell pepper, diced
- 2 cloves garlic, minced
- 1 cup short-grain or paella rice
- 1/2 teaspoon saffron threads
- 1/2 teaspoon smoked paprika
- 1/2 teaspoon ground cumin
- 1/2 cup white wine (optional)
- 1 1/2 cups chicken broth
- 1/2 cup (2.5 oz) frozen peas
- 1 small tomato, diced
- Salt and black pepper, to taste
- Lemon wedges, for serving
- Fresh parsley, chopped (for garnish)

Prepare Time:

15 Minutes

Cook Time:

30 Minutes

Total Time:

45 Minutes

Serving:

2

Instructions

- In a large, deep skillet or paella pan, heat the olive oil over medium heat.

- Add the chicken pieces to the pan and cook until browned on all sides, about 5-7 minutes. Remove the chicken from the pan and set aside.

- Add the sliced chorizo to the pan and cook until it begins to release its oils, about 3 minutes. Remove the chorizo and set aside with the chicken.

- In the same pan, add the chopped onion and red bell pepper. Sauté until softened, about 5 minutes.

- Stir in the minced garlic and cook for an additional 1 minute until fragrant.

- Stir in the rice, saffron threads, smoked paprika, and ground cumin. Cook for 1-2 minutes, allowing the rice to toast slightly and absorb the spices.

- If using, pour in the white wine and let it cook for 2 minutes, scraping up any browned bits from the bottom of the pan.

- Add the chicken broth, frozen peas, and diced tomato. Stir to combine. Return the cooked chicken and chorizo to the pan. Add salt and pepper to taste, bring to a simmer, then reduce heat to low.

- Cover the pan and cook for 20-25 minutes, or until the rice is tender and has absorbed the liquid. Avoid stirring during this time to allow the rice to form the crispy socarrat on the bottom.

- Once cooked, remove from heat and let the paella sit, covered, for 5 minutes. Garnish with chopped fresh parsley and serve with lemon wedges on the side.

Tried & True Tips & Hacks

Saffron Substitution: If saffron is hard to find or too pricey, you can use a pinch of turmeric for color and a milder flavor.

Rice Choice: Use short-grain or paella rice for the best texture. If you can't find these, Arborio rice is a good substitute.

Avoid Stirring: Once you add the liquid, avoid stirring the rice. This helps in developing the traditional crispy bottom layer.

Customize: Feel free to add other vegetables like green beans or artichokes, or swap out the chicken for seafood if preferred.

Leftovers

Paella: Store leftover paella in an airtight container in the refrigerator. It will keep well for up to 3 days. If you have a lot of leftovers, consider portioning them into smaller containers to make reheating easier. Reheat leftover paella in a skillet over medium heat. Add a splash of water or chicken broth to help rehydrate the rice and prevent it from drying out. Cover the skillet to trap moisture, and stir occasionally until heated through. Avoid using the microwave if you want to preserve the socarrat, as it can become mushy.

Chicken and Chorizo: Leftover chicken and chorizo offer great versatility and can be repurposed into a variety of delicious dishes. Add chopped chicken and chorizo to a beaten egg mixture and cook in a skillet to make a savory omelet. Top with cheese and fresh herbs for added flavor. Or make chicken and chorizo pizza by spreading pizza dough with tomato sauce or olive oil, topping with cheese, and scattering the chicken and chorizo over the top. Bake until the crust is crispy and the cheese is melted.

Cooking Together

Mastering the Art of Waiting

Understand the Technique: Cooking paella requires patience. Once you add the liquid to the rice, it's crucial to let it simmer undisturbed. Stirring or moving the rice too much can prevent the socarrat from forming. This crispy, caramelized layer at the bottom is a hallmark of great paella, and achieving it requires a bit of trust in the process. Just like in relationships, if you ask me.

Embrace the Wait: While waiting for the paella to cook, use this time to chat and enjoy each other's company. The anticipation of that crispy bottom layer makes the meal even more rewarding.

Resist the Urge: Avoid the temptation to lift the lid too frequently. Letting the paella cook on low heat without disturbing it will help develop the rich flavors and create the delightful texture that defines a perfect paella.

Play a Spanish Food Game

Game Setup: To add a fun element to your cooking time, play a game where each person describes a Spanish food they love while the other guesses the name. This game can be a great way to bond and discover new favorites.

How to Play:

One Describes: One person starts by describing a Spanish dish, mentioning its ingredients, texture, or unique characteristics without saying the name of the dish.

The Other Guesses: The other person listens carefully and tries to guess what dish is being described. You can make it competitive or just for fun, depending on your mood.

Examples to Describe:

Tortilla Española: "This is a Spanish omelet made with potatoes and onions, cooked in a pan and often enjoyed at room temperature."

Gazpacho: "A refreshing cold soup made from tomatoes, cucumbers, peppers, and garlic, perfect for a hot day."

Churros: "Fried dough pastries that are often enjoyed for breakfast or as a dessert, usually served with a cup of thick hot chocolate."

I'm not going to take sides, but I hope you win!

MAIN COURSES

Spanish Tortilla with Spinach and Goat Cheese

Watching someone attempt to flip a tortilla or omelet is one of those simple pleasures that brings a smile to my face every time. There's something undeniably captivating about that moment of truth—when the pan is lifted, and the delicate dance of flipping takes place. It's a move that makes everyone truly and beautifully vulnerable as they hold their breath and hope for the best outcome. It's not just about cooking; it's about embracing the unpredictability and the joy that comes with it.

That's precisely why I had to include this Spanish Tortilla with Spinach and Goat Cheese in this book. It's a dish that embodies both the art of cooking and the charm of those authentic kitchen moments. When you attempt to flip this tortilla, you're engaging in a tradition that has been cherished in kitchens across Spain for generations. It's a small act that can lead to big laughs and shared stories, making the meal not just about the food but about the experience itself.

And if you're looking to add a bit more substance to your tortilla, you're in luck. This dish is wonderfully adaptable. For added protein, you can mix in ingredients like diced chicken or turkey, which will seamlessly blend with the potatoes, spinach, and goat cheese. Chorizo adds a smoky kick and extra protein, infusing the tortilla with a rich, savory depth. If you're a fan of ham, diced or shredded ham works beautifully as well, providing a classic and hearty flavor.

So, as you prepare this tortilla, enjoy the process—embrace the flip, savor the laughter, and relish the delicious outcome. Whether you're adding extra protein or keeping it simple, this recipe is designed to be both versatile and memorable, capturing the essence of Spanish home cooking and the joy of creating something special together.

Ingredients For Two

For the Tortilla

- 1 tablespoon extra virgin olive oil
- 2 medium potatoes, peeled and thinly sliced (about 1/8 inch thick)
- 1 small onion, finely chopped
- 2 cloves garlic, minced
- 1/2 cup (2.5 oz) fresh spinach, roughly chopped
- 4 large eggs
- Salt and black pepper, to taste
- 2 oz goat cheese, crumbled

For Serving (Optional)

- Fresh herbs (like parsley or chives), chopped
- Extra goat cheese, crumbled

Prepare Time:
15 Minutes

Cook Time:
25 Minutes

Total Time:
45 Minutes

Serving:
2

Instructions

- Heat the olive oil in a non-stick skillet over medium heat. Add the sliced potatoes and cook, stirring occasionally, until they are tender and lightly golden, about 15 minutes. You may need to adjust the heat to prevent burning.

- Once the potatoes are cooked, remove them from the skillet and drain on paper towels. Season with a little salt and pepper.

- In the same skillet, add a little more olive oil if needed. Sauté the onion until softened and translucent, about 5 minutes.

- Add the minced garlic and cook for another minute until fragrant.

- Add the chopped spinach and cook until wilted, about 2-3 minutes. Remove from heat.

- In a large bowl, whisk together the eggs. Season with salt and pepper.

- Fold in the cooked potatoes, sautéed spinach and onion, and crumbled goat cheese.

- Wipe the skillet clean and heat a little olive oil over medium heat. Pour the egg mixture into the skillet, spreading it evenly.

- Cook without stirring for about 6-8 minutes, or until the edges start to set and the bottom is golden brown. You can use a spatula to gently lift the edges to check for browning.

- To flip the tortilla, place a large plate over the skillet and carefully invert the tortilla onto the plate. Then, slide the tortilla back into the skillet, cooked side up.

- Cook for an additional 4-5 minutes, or until the tortilla is fully set and golden brown on both sides.

- Slide the tortilla onto a cutting board and let it cool for a few minutes before slicing.

- Garnish with additional crumbled goat cheese and fresh herbs if desired. Serve warm or at room temperature.

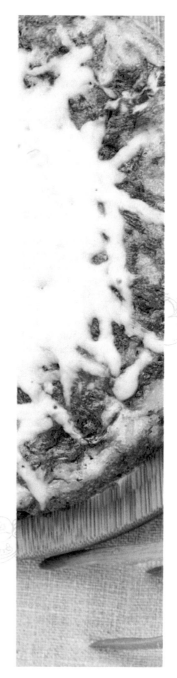

Tried & True Tips & Hacks

Uniform Slicing: For even cooking, try to slice the potatoes uniformly. A mandoline slicer can help achieve consistent thickness.

Taste and Adjust: Before adding the egg mixture to the skillet, taste a small amount of the potato and spinach mixture. This will help you adjust the seasoning with salt and pepper, ensuring your tortilla has the right flavor balance.

Non-Stick Skillet: Use a non-stick skillet to make flipping the tortilla easier and to prevent sticking.

Low and Slow: Cook the tortilla over medium to low heat. This allows the eggs to set slowly, ensuring the tortilla cooks evenly without burning the bottom. It also helps in achieving a tender texture throughout.

Use a Large Plate: To flip the tortilla, place a large plate over the skillet, then carefully invert the skillet to transfer the tortilla to the plate. Slide the tortilla back into the skillet with the cooked side up. This method helps you flip it without breaking it into pieces.

Cooling: Allow the tortilla to cool slightly before slicing. This helps it set and makes it easier to cut into neat slices.

Variations: Feel free to add other ingredients like bell peppers, tomatoes, or herbs to customize your tortilla

Leftovers

Leftover Tortilla: Store leftover Spanish Tortilla in an airtight container in the refrigerator. It will keep well for up to 3 days. For longer storage, you can freeze individual slices in a freezer-safe container for up to 2 months.

Reheating

Skillet: Reheat slices in a non-stick skillet over medium-low heat. This helps to maintain the tortilla's crispy texture. Cover with a lid or foil to heat evenly and prevent the edges from burning.

Oven: Alternatively, you can reheat the tortilla in the oven. Place slices on a baking sheet and cover with foil. Heat at 350°F (175°C) for about 10-15 minutes or until warmed through.

Avoid Microwaving: While convenient, microwaving can make the tortilla soggy. If you must use a microwave, heat in short intervals and place a paper towel between the tortilla and the microwave plate to absorb excess moisture.

Spanish Tortilla with Spinach and Goat Cheese Leftovers

Tortilla Wraps: Use leftover tortilla slices as a filling for wraps. Add fresh vegetables, a spread like hummus, or extra protein for a quick and satisfying meal.

Tortilla Salad: Dice the leftover tortilla and toss with fresh greens, tomatoes, cucumbers, and a light vinaigrette to make a hearty salad.

Tortilla Frittata: Incorporate leftover tortilla into a frittata. Chop it into pieces and mix with beaten eggs and other vegetables before baking.

Cooking Together

Mastering the Flip: The flip is often the most anticipated moment when making a tortilla. Encourage each other and share tips on how to achieve the perfect flip. Remember, it's all part of the fun and learning process. The more you practice, the better you'll get, and the more confident you'll become.

Prepare Together: Work together to prep the ingredients. One person can peel and slice the potatoes while the other handles the spinach and goat cheese. This not only speeds up the process but also makes it a shared activity.

Cooking in Tandem: As you cook the tortilla, take turns handling different tasks. One person can manage the stove while the other sets the table or prepares side dishes. It keeps things moving smoothly and makes the experience more enjoyable.

Sample as You Go: Taste the potato and spinach mixture before adding it to the eggs. It's a great way to ensure the seasoning is just right and gives you a chance to discuss flavor preferences and adjustments together.

Celebrate the Small Wins: Whether the flip is flawless or a little less perfect, celebrate the effort. The joy of cooking together comes from the experience, not just the final product. Share a laugh over any mishaps and appreciate the creativity and teamwork involved.

Set the Scene: Once the tortilla is cooked and ready to serve, set the table together. Add some fresh herbs or extra goat cheese for garnish and enjoy the fruits of your labor. Eating together and sharing the meal you've prepared can be the most rewarding part of the cooking process.

Reflect on the Experience: Take a moment to reflect on what went well and what you learned during the cooking process. Discuss any new techniques or tips you discovered and how they can be applied to future cooking adventures.

DESSERT

Churros with Chocolate Dipping Sauce

A Sweet Finale! The moment we've all been waiting for has finally arrived—the rich, velvety chocolate dipping sauce is ready to elevate our homemade churros to new heights of indulgence. Imagine the excitement as you take those crispy, cinnamon-sugar-coated churros and dip them into the warm, decadent chocolate sauce. It's a moment that turns an already amazing treat into a truly memorable experience.

It's not just about the taste; it's about the joy of sharing a sweet moment together. So, gather around, dip generously, and relish every bite of this perfect pairing. This is the sweet reward that makes all the effort and fun of making churros together truly worth it.

Ingredients For Two

For the Churros

- 1/2 cup water
- 1/4 cup unsalted butter
- 2 tablespoons granulated sugar
- 1/4 teaspoon salt
- 1/2 cup all-purpose flour
- 1 medium egg
- 1/2 teaspoon vanilla extract
- Vegetable oil, for frying

For the Cinnamon Sugar Coating

- 1/4 cup granulated sugar
- 1 teaspoon ground cinnamon
- For the Chocolate Dipping Sauce
- 1/2 cup heavy cream
- 1/2 cup (3 oz) semi-sweet chocolate chips
- 1/2 teaspoon vanilla extract

Prepare Time:
15 Minutes

Cook Time:
20 Minutes

Total Time:
35 Minutes

Serving:
2 (approximately 6)

Instructions

Churros Dough

- In a small saucepan, combine the water, butter, sugar, and salt. Bring to a boil over medium heat, stirring until the butter is melted and the sugar is dissolved.
- Remove from heat and stir in the flour until the mixture forms a thick paste. Return to low heat and cook, stirring constantly, for about 1-2 minutes to dry out the dough slightly.
- Transfer the dough to a mixing bowl and let it cool for about 5 minutes. Once cooled, beat in the egg and vanilla extract until smooth and well combined.
- In a deep skillet or saucepan, heat about 2 inches of vegetable oil to 350°F (175°C). Use a thermometer to monitor the temperature.

Cinnamon Sugar Coating

- In a small bowl, mix together the granulated sugar and ground cinnamon. Set aside.
- Transfer the churro dough to a piping bag fitted with a large star tip. Carefully pipe 4-inch long strips of dough into the hot oil, cutting them with scissors or a knife.
- Fry the churros in batches, making sure not to overcrowd the pan. Cook for about 2-3 minutes on each side, or until golden brown and crispy. Use a slotted spoon to remove the churros from the oil and drain on paper towels.
- While still warm, roll the churros in the cinnamon sugar mixture until evenly coated.

Chocolate Dipping Sauce

- In a small saucepan, heat the heavy cream over medium heat until it just begins to simmer.
- Remove from heat and stir in the chocolate chips until melted and smooth. Stir in the vanilla extract. Serve the churros warm with the chocolate dipping sauce on the side.

Tried & True Tips & Hacks

Perfect Oil Temperature: Keeping the oil at the right temperature is crucial. If it's too hot, the churros will burn on the outside before cooking through. If it's too cool, they will be greasy and soggy. Use a thermometer for best results.

Pipe in Batches: Don't overcrowd the pan. Fry churros in batches to ensure they cook evenly and become crispy.

Cooling the Dough: Allowing the dough to cool slightly before adding the egg helps prevent scrambling the egg, leading to a smoother texture.

Customize the Coating: Experiment with different spices like nutmeg or cardamom in the cinnamon sugar coating for a unique twist.

Leftovers

Leftover Churros: Store leftover churros in an airtight container at room temperature for up to 2 days. For longer storage, freeze churros in a single layer on a baking sheet, then transfer to a freezer-safe bag. They can be frozen for up to 2 months.

Reheating

Oven: Preheat your oven to 350°F (175°C). Place churros on a baking sheet and reheat for about 10 minutes or until warmed through and crispy. This method helps maintain their texture.

Air Fryer: If you have an air fryer, preheat it to 350°F (175°C) and reheat churros for about 5 minutes. This can help them regain their original crispiness.

Avoid Microwaving: Microwaving churros can make them soggy. If you must use a microwave, reheat in short intervals and place a paper towel between the churros and the microwave plate to absorb excess moisture.

Chocolate Dipping Sauce: Store leftover chocolate sauce in an airtight container in the refrigerator for up to 1 week. For longer storage, it can be frozen in a freezer-safe container for up to 2 months.

Reheating

Stovetop: Reheat the sauce gently over low heat in a saucepan, stirring frequently until smooth and warm.

Microwave: Reheat in short intervals (15-20 seconds) in the microwave, stirring after each interval to ensure even heating.

Creative Uses for Leftovers

Churro Crumbs: If your churros become a bit stale, break them into crumbs and use them as a topping for ice cream, yogurt, or dessert parfaits. They can also be blended into a crumbly coating for baked goods.

Chocolate Sauce Uses: Use leftover chocolate sauce as a topping for pancakes, waffles, or ice cream. It can also be stirred into coffee for a mocha flavor or drizzled fruit for a decadent treat.

Cooking Together

Team Up for Prep: Assign different tasks to each person. One can handle mixing and preparing the churro dough while the other heats the oil and sets up the cinnamon sugar coating.

Prep Together: Measure and mix the ingredients together. This not only speeds up the process but also allows you to enjoy the preparation as a shared activity.

Take Turns Frying: Fry the churros in batches and take turns managing the frying process. This gives everyone a chance to get involved and learn the art of frying.

Celebrate Successes: Whether the churros turn out perfectly or have a few imperfections, celebrate the effort and enjoy the process. Laughter and camaraderie make the experience memorable.

Play a Food-Themed Game: Churro Trivia! While you wait for the churros to fry or the chocolate sauce to heat, play a food-themed trivia game. Each person takes turns asking questions about Spanish cuisine or churros, and the other person guesses the answers.

DRINK

Tinto de Verano

I like to think of this recipe as an "Effortlessly Chic Wine for the Modern Palate." For those who adore the concept of wine but sometimes find it a bit overwhelming, Tinto de Verano is your perfect match. Imagine sangria with a touch of sophistication—it's like sangria that went to college and now wears designer clothes, but in the most effortless, chic way. This refreshing Spanish drink is light and fruity, a seamless blend of red wine and zesty lemon soda that exudes elegance without any fuss.

It's ideal for those who appreciate the depth of wine but crave a more approachable, laid-back experience. Whether you're relaxing on a sunny afternoon or sharing a casual evening with friends, Tinto de Verano provides all the charm of wine with a refreshing twist. So, raise your glass to a drink that's stylishly uncomplicated, and enjoy a taste of Spain!

Ingredients For Two

- 1 cup red wine (choose a fruity, light red wine like Tempranillo or Garnacha)
- 1 cup lemon soda (or club soda with a splash of lemon juice for a lighter option)
- Ice cubes
- Lemon slices (for garnish)
- Fresh mint leaves (optional, for garnish)

Prepare Time:
5 Minutes

Total Time:
5 Minutes

Serving:
2

Instructions

- For the best taste, chill the red wine and lemon soda before preparing the drink.

- In a large pitcher or mixing glass, combine the red wine and lemon soda. Stir gently to mix.

- Taste the mixture and adjust the ratio of wine to soda if desired. For a lighter, more refreshing drink, add more lemon soda.

- Fill two glasses with ice cubes.

- Pour the Tinto de Verano over the ice. Garnish each glass with a lemon slice and, if using, a few fresh mint leaves.

- Serve immediately and enjoy the refreshing flavors of your Tinto de Verano.

Tried & True Tips & Hacks

Wine Choice: Use a light and fruity red wine to complement the citrus flavors. Avoid overly tannic or heavy wines, as they can overpower the drink.

Customize: Adjust the sweetness by varying the amount of lemon soda. You can also use flavored sodas or add a splash of fruit juice for a twist.

Make Ahead: You can prepare the Tinto de Verano in advance, but keep the wine and soda separate until just before serving to maintain the fizz.

Lemon Juice: If you prefer to use club soda instead of lemon soda, add a splash of fresh lemon juice for that extra zesty kick.

Leftovers

Red Wine: Use leftover red wine in sauces, stews, or marinades to add depth of flavor. Or simmer the wine to reduce it into a flavorful glaze or reduction for meats and vegetables.

Lemon Soda: Use leftover lemon soda as a mixer for other cocktails or mocktails. Or even better, reduce the soda to make a lemon syrup that can be used in desserts or as a topping for pancakes and waffles.

Lemon Juice: Use lemon juice in salad dressings or marinades. You can also add it to baked goods for a fresh lemon flavor or use it to brighten up dishes like soups, stews, and sauces.

Cooking Together

Chill Together: If the wine and soda are not yet chilled, take this opportunity to discuss their flavors and decide how to adjust the drink to your taste preferences.

Garnish Together: Slice the lemons and, if using, prepare the mint leaves. Add these garnishes to the glasses for a touch of elegance and extra flavor

Hopefully, you are enjoying the latest cookbook by Louise Mayfield. Please check out her entire collection on Amazon by scanning the QR code below.

CHAPTER 5
TURKEY

"işten artmaz, dişten artar"

"Savings don't come from what you earn, but from what you don't waste."

In Turkey, the act of finishing every last morsel on your plate isn't just about good manners—it's a deeply ingrained cultural and religious practice. Turks believe that leaving food behind is not just wasteful but a sin, rooted in religious law that emphasizes the importance of avoiding waste. This is why, in Turkish households, scraping the bottom of the plate and ensuring nothing is left uneaten is a common practice.

For Turks, home-cooked meals hold a special place in their hearts, far surpassing the offerings of any restaurant. The reasons for this preference are simple yet profound: cleanliness, the care and love poured into each dish, superior flavor, and the economy of making meals at home. In Turkish culture, it's not just about the food on the plate; it's about the love and effort that went into preparing it.

Interestingly, talking about what you've eaten is considered distasteful in Turkish culture. Boasting about a meal is frowned upon, as what is enjoyed within the privacy of one's home is not meant to be shared outside. This respect for the sanctity of home extends to the unspoken rule that when a guest arrives, they must be fed, no matter the circumstances. Whether expected or not, a guest is welcomed with whatever is available, perfectly captured by the saying, "The guest eats what he finds, not what he hopes for."

In Turkish rural areas, this hospitality shines even brighter, with food always ready to be shared. And within these homes, the phrase "işten artmaz, dişten artar" resonates strongly. This expression underscores the necessity of avoiding waste and practicing frugality, particularly in the kitchen. It's a reminder that savings aren't made by cutting corners on work but by being mindful of what we consume—ensuring that leftovers never go to waste but are creatively reused the next day. Which is precisely what I aim to do in this cookbook, in this chapter, and in life in general.

This chapter on Turkish cuisine embraces the spirit of "işten artmaz, dişten artar," tying together the principles of frugality, respect for food, and the importance of home-cooked meals. Designed for two, these recipes minimize waste and encourage the thoughtful use of leftovers. Each dish reflects the Turkish way of life—where every meal is prepared with care, enjoyed to the last bite, and creatively repurposed, ensuring nothing is wasted. In the process, you'll not only discover the rich flavors of Turkey but also the deep cultural values that make its cuisine so special.

SALAD

Pomegranate and Walnut Salad

Turkey is one of the motherlands of the pomegranate, a fruit that holds deep cultural significance in the region. In Turkish culture, the pomegranate is far more than just a delicious fruit; it is a powerful symbol of good fortune, abundance, and fertility. This rich symbolism is why I couldn't leave this vibrant ingredient out of this chapter.

The pomegranate's place in Turkish tradition is steeped in history and lore. It is said that only a century ago, pomegranates were used as a metaphor in marriage proposals. The story goes that when a man wished to propose to a woman, he would send her a basket of pomegranates as a gift. The gesture was laden with meaning, symbolizing a hopeful future filled with prosperity, health, and many children.

In creating this Pomegranate and Walnut Salad, I was inspired by this tradition. While I'm not proposing marriage, I am proposing something equally delightful: diving into this delicious salad together. It's more than just a dish—it's an invitation to savor the beauty of sharing a healthy meal, rich in symbolism and flavor. So, as you enjoy the sweet burst of pomegranate seeds, the crunch of toasted walnuts, and the creaminess of feta, remember the history and significance of this incredible fruit. Here's to good fortune, abundance, and the joy of sharing a meal with someone special.

Ingredients For Two

For the Pomegranate Molasses Dressing

- 2 tablespoons pomegranate molasses
- 1 tablespoon extra virgin olive oil
- 1 teaspoon balsamic vinegar
- 1 teaspoon honey (optional, for added sweetness)
- Salt and pepper to taste

For the Salad

- 4 cups mixed greens (such as arugula, spinach, and romaine)
- 1/2 cup pomegranate seeds
- 1/4 cup toasted walnuts, roughly chopped
- 1/4 cup crumbled feta cheese

Prepare Time:
10 Minutes

Total Time:
10 Minutes

Serving:
2

Instructions

For the Dressing

- In a small bowl, whisk together the pomegranate molasses, olive oil, balsamic vinegar, and honey (if using). Season with salt and pepper to taste. Adjust the sweetness or tanginess by adding more honey or vinegar as needed.

For the Salad

- In a large bowl, combine the mixed greens, pomegranate seeds, and toasted walnuts.
- Drizzle the pomegranate molasses dressing over the salad. Toss gently to ensure the greens are evenly coated with the dressing.
- Sprinkle the crumbled feta cheese over the top of the salad.
- Divide the salad between two plates. Serve immediately and enjoy the mix of sweet, tangy, and crunchy flavors.

Tried & True Tips & Hacks

Easily Extract Pomegranate Seeds: To avoid the mess that comes with extracting pomegranate seeds, cut the pomegranate in half, then hold each half over a bowl and tap the back with a wooden spoon. The seeds will fall out easily without staining your hands. And it makes a pretty funny sound. Try it.

Pre-Toasted Walnuts: Save time by purchasing pre-toasted walnuts from the store. If you prefer to toast them yourself, do it in bulk and store them in an airtight container for up to two weeks. This way, you'll have toasted nuts ready to sprinkle on salads or use in other dishes.

Customize Your Dressing: If you find the dressing too tangy, balance it by adding a touch more honey. Conversely, if you prefer more acidity, increase the balsamic vinegar. This dressing is versatile and can be adjusted to suit your taste.

Keep Your Greens Crisp: If you're preparing the salad ahead of time, store the mixed greens in a bowl lined with paper towels to absorb moisture and keep them fresh. Dress the salad just before serving to prevent the greens from wilting.

Add Protein: For a more substantial meal, add a protein source like grilled chicken, shrimp, or even a handful of chickpeas. This turns the salad into a complete, balanced dish that's perfect for lunch or a light dinner.

Leftovers

Pomegranate Seeds: Sprinkle leftover pomegranate seeds over yogurt, oatmeal, or cereal for a burst of sweetness and color in your morning routine. Or, add them to sparkling water or cocktails for a refreshing and visually appealing garnish.

Toasted Walnuts: Enjoy toasted walnuts as a healthy snack on their own or mix them into a homemade trail mix with dried fruits and other nuts. You can also use them in baked goods like muffins, banana bread, or cookies for added crunch and flavor.

Feta Cheese: Crumble leftover feta into an omelet or scrambled eggs for a tangy, savory twist. Then, you can also consider using it to stuff bell peppers, tomatoes, or mushrooms along with herbs and breadcrumbs for a quick and tasty dish. Or you can move on to the next recipe in this book and use it up to make Sigara Böreği.
Pomegranate Molasses Dressing: Use the leftover dressing as a marinade for chicken, lamb, or tofu. The tangy and slightly sweet flavor works beautifully with grilled meats. If you are not a meat lover, you can drizzle it over roasted vegetables like carrots, beets, or Brussels sprouts for an extra layer of flavor.

Cooking Together

Divide and Conquer: While one person washes and preps the greens, the other can handle extracting the pomegranate seeds or toasting the walnuts. This division of tasks keeps things moving smoothly and ensures you're working together as a team.

Create a Flavor Station: Set up a small station with the ingredients for the pomegranate molasses dressing. One person can measure and whisk the dressing while the other tastes and adjusts the seasoning. This is a great way to collaborate and learn each other's flavor preferences.

Presentation Matters: Take turns arranging the salad on plates. One person can be in charge of placing the greens, while the other artistically sprinkles the pomegranate seeds, walnuts, and feta. Make it a fun competition to see who can create the most visually appealing plate!

Toast to Your Efforts: Once the salad is ready, take a moment to appreciate your teamwork. Pour a glass of wine or sparkling water, and toast to the delicious meal you've created together. This simple act can make the experience even more enjoyable and memorable.

Play a Game: While cooking, try a fun game where one of you describes a favorite dish or ingredient without naming it, and the other guesses what it is. This adds a playful element to your cooking session and keeps the conversation lively.

APPETIZER

Sigara Böreği (Feta-Stuffed Phyllo Cigars)

This recipe for Sigara Böreği draws inspiration from the traditional Turkish version, which is made with delicate, paper-thin sheets of dough called Yufka and filled with Lor cheese—a mild white cheese—or beyaz peynir, a classic Turkish white cheese. To make this recipe more accessible, I've adapted it using phyllo dough and feta cheese, ingredients that are easy to find and work beautifully together. This simplified version is perfect for two, with minimal leftovers, and any extras can be easily incorporated into other dishes in the book.

Sigara Böreği makes a fantastic starter, especially when paired with other meze dishes to create a full Turkish-style menu. They're also great for meal prep, holding up well in the fridge, and they make a delicious addition to a packed lunch. Whether you're sharing them as a snack or incorporating them into a larger meal, these crispy, savory pastries are a must-try!

Ingredients For Two

For the Böreği

- 1/2 cup feta cheese, crumbled
- 1 tablespoon fresh parsley, finely chopped
- 1 tablespoon fresh dill, finely chopped
- Salt and pepper, to taste
- 4 sheets of phyllo dough
- 1/4 cup unsalted butter, melted (or extra virgin olive oil for brushing)
- 1 egg yolk (for sealing the edges)

For the Yogurt Dipping Sauce

- 1/2 cup plain Greek yogurt
- 1 clove garlic, minced
- 1 tablespoon lemon juice
- 1 tablespoon fresh mint, finely chopped (optional)
- Salt and pepper, to taste

✓ **Prepare Time:**	10 Minutes
✓ **Cook Time:**	20 minutes
✓ **Total Time:**	35 minutes
✓ **Serving:**	2 (Makes about 8 cigars)

Instructions

For the Böreği

- In a small bowl, mix the crumbled feta cheese with the chopped parsley and dill. Season with a little salt and pepper to taste (be mindful of the saltiness of the feta).
- Preheat your oven to 375°F (190°C) and line a baking sheet with parchment paper.
- Carefully lay out one sheet of phyllo dough on a clean, flat surface. Keep the remaining phyllo sheets covered with a damp cloth to prevent them from drying out.
- Brush the phyllo sheet lightly with melted butter or olive oil. Place another sheet on top and repeat the brushing. Cut the stacked phyllo sheets into 4 equal rectangles.
- Place about 1 tablespoon of the feta mixture at the end of each phyllo rectangle.
- Fold the sides over the filling and then roll the phyllo tightly into a cigar shape. Brush a little egg yolk on the end of the phyllo to seal the roll. Repeat the process with the remaining phyllo sheets and filling.
- Place the phyllo cigars on the prepared baking sheet. Brush the tops lightly with more melted butter or olive oil.
- Bake in the preheated oven for 15-20 minutes, or until golden brown and crispy.

For the Yogurt Dipping Sauce

- While the böreği are baking, mix the Greek yogurt, minced garlic, lemon juice, and fresh mint (if using) in a small bowl. Season with salt and pepper to taste.
- Once baked, allow the böreği to cool slightly before serving. Serve them warm with the yogurt dipping sauce on the side.

Tried & True Tips & Hacks

Prevent Phyllo from Drying Out: Phyllo dough dries out quickly, so keep the sheets you're not working with covered with a damp cloth. This will help prevent them from becoming brittle and difficult to handle.

Easy Filling Distribution: To make sure each böreği has the perfect amount of filling, divide your feta mixture into equal portions before you start assembling. This way, you won't run out of filling or end up with uneven rolls.

Sealing the Rolls: Use a little egg yolk or water to seal the edges of the phyllo dough tightly. This helps prevent the filling from leaking out during baking and ensures the rolls stay crispy and intact.

Get Creative with Fillings: While feta and herbs are traditional, you can experiment with other fillings like spinach, caramelized onions, or even ground meat. Just be sure to keep the filling dry to avoid soggy phyllo.

Bake, Don't Fry: While Sigara Böreği are traditionally fried, baking them gives you a lighter, less greasy version that's just as crispy and delicious. Plus, it's easier and less messy.

Make-Ahead Option: These böreği can be assembled ahead of time and frozen before baking. When you're ready to enjoy them, simply bake from frozen, adding a few extra minutes to the cooking time.

Perfect Pairing: Serve with a tangy yogurt dip or a squeeze of lemon for added brightness and a touch of acidity that complements the rich, savory flavors of the böreği.

Leftovers

Feta Cheese

Greek Salad: Use leftover feta to whip up a refreshing Greek Salad with tomatoes, cucumbers, olives, and red onions. The perfect recipe awaits in the Greek chapter of this book.

Pomegranate and Walnut Salad: Crumble the feta over the Pomegranate and Walnut Salad from this Turkish chapter for added creaminess and flavor.

Stuffed Peppers: Mix feta with cooked quinoa or rice, herbs, and veggies to make a filling for stuffed peppers. Bake until tender for a light and satisfying meal.

Scrambled Eggs or Omelets: Stir crumbled feta into scrambled eggs or an omelet for a creamy, tangy boost.

Phyllo Dough

Baklava: Use leftover phyllo to make a sweet and sticky Baklava from the Greek chapter, layering the sheets with nuts and honey.

Mini Quiches: Create mini phyllo quiches by pressing the dough into muffin tins, filling it with eggs, cheese, and vegetables, and baking until golden.

Phyllo Pie: Use the phyllo to make a savory pie, such as Spanakopita, by turning back to the Greek chapter of this cookbook and layering it with spinach and feta filling.

Fruit Turnovers: Cut the phyllo into squares, fill with fruit compote, and fold into triangles to create quick fruit turnovers that are perfect for dessert or breakfast.

Herbs (Parsley, Dill, Mint)

Tabbouleh: Use leftover parsley to make a fresh tabbouleh salad with bulgur, tomatoes, and lemon juice. Herb Butter: Mix the herbs with softened butter and garlic, then chill to create a flavorful herb butter for spreading on bread or melting over grilled meats.

Smoothies: Toss leftover mint or parsley into a green smoothie for a fresh and nutritious boost. In my recipe for the perfect Turkish Mint Lemonade, you'll find another creative way to use up the whole bunch of mint, guilt-free!

Cooking Together

Divide and Conquer: Cooking Sigara Böreği together is a fun way to divide tasks. One person can prepare the filling while the other handles the phyllo dough. Working together makes the process quicker and more enjoyable, plus it gives you a chance to chat and share stories while you cook.

Rolling Challenge: Turn the assembly of Sigara Böreği into a friendly competition. See who can roll the tightest, most perfect cigars, and who can make the most without tearing the phyllo. It's a lighthearted way to add some fun to your cooking session.

Cultural Exploration: While you wait for the böreği to bake, take a moment to explore Turkish culture together. Look up Turkish music or watch a short documentary about Turkish cuisine to enhance the experience and set the mood.

Packed Lunches with an Ethnic Spin: After making a batch of Sigara Böreği, why not prepare packed lunches for each other? Wrap up a few of these savory pastries, add a small container of yogurt sauce, and perhaps a side of olives or a salad. It's a thoughtful and delicious way to surprise each other the next day, and it adds an ethnic spin to your lunch routine.

Meze Platter: For dinner, create a meze platter together by combining the Sigara Böreği with other small dishes like hummus, stuffed grape leaves, and olives. It's a fun way to try a variety of flavors and enjoy a meal that's meant to be shared.

Learn Together: If you're both new to working with phyllo dough, take it as an opportunity to learn together. Be patient with the process, and don't worry if your first few rolls aren't perfect—they'll still taste delicious! Celebrate your successes and laugh off any imperfections.

MAIN COURSES

Lamb Köfte with Yogurt Sauce

When you think of Turkish cuisine, the mind often drifts to images of döner kebabs or sizzling skewers, but there's another dish that holds an even more cherished place in Turkish hearts: köfte. These succulent meat patties, while similar to meatballs, are anything but ordinary. Across Turkey, there are countless regional variations of köfte, each with its own unique blend of spices and preparation methods, making it one of the most beloved and widely consumed dishes in the country. Among these, the classic homemade köfte stands out. It's the kind that's lovingly prepared by mothers and grandmothers, each with their own secret recipe passed down through generations. This recipe is exactly that.

Ingredients For Two

For the Lamb Köfte

- 9 oz ground lamb
- 1 garlic clove, minced
- 1 small onion, finely grated
- 1 tablespoon fresh parsley, finely chopped
- 1 tablespoon fresh mint, finely chopped
- 1 teaspoon ground cumin
- 1 teaspoon ground coriander
- 1/2 teaspoon ground paprika
- 1/4 teaspoon ground cinnamon
- 1/4 teaspoon chili flakes (optional)
- Salt and pepper, to taste
- 1 tablespoon olive oil, for cooking

For the Yogurt Sauce

- 1/2 cup plain Greek yogurt
- 1 garlic clove, minced
- 1 tablespoon fresh mint, finely chopped
- 1 teaspoon lemon juice
- Salt and pepper, to taste
- Optional Garnishes
- Fresh parsley or mint leaves
- A drizzle of olive oil

✓ **Prepare Time:**	15 Minutes
✓ **Cook Time:**	15 minutes
✓ **Total Time:**	30 minutes
✓ **Serving:**	2

Instructions

For the Köfte Mixture

- In a mixing bowl, combine the ground lamb, minced garlic, grated onion, parsley, mint, cumin, coriander, paprika, cinnamon, chili flakes, salt, and pepper.
- Mix thoroughly until all the ingredients are well incorporated. Using your hands, shape the mixture into small patties or logs about 2-3 inches in length.
- Heat a tablespoon of olive oil in a large skillet over medium-high heat. Once the oil is hot, add the lamb köfte to the skillet.
- Cook for 3-4 minutes on each side, or until they are nicely browned on the outside and cooked through. The köfte should reach an internal temperature of 160°F (71°C) for medium doneness.

For the Yogurt Sauce

- While the köfte are cooking, prepare the yogurt sauce. In a small bowl, mix together the Greek yogurt, minced garlic, chopped mint, lemon juice, salt, and pepper.
- Stir well to combine and set aside.
- Once the köfte are cooked, remove them from the skillet and let them rest for a minute. Serve the köfte warm with the yogurt sauce on the side.
- Garnish with additional fresh mint or parsley and a drizzle of olive oil, if desired.

Tried & True Tips & Hacks

Rest the Mixture: After mixing the ground lamb with spices and herbs, let the mixture rest in the refrigerator for at least 30 minutes. This allows the flavors to meld together and makes the mixture easier to shape.

Moisten Your Hands: Before shaping the köfte, wet your hands slightly with water or a bit of olive oil. This prevents the meat mixture from sticking to your hands and helps you achieve smooth, even shapes.

Crispy Köfte: If you prefer a crispy exterior, coat the köfte lightly in breadcrumbs before frying. This adds an extra layer of texture that contrasts beautifully with the tender lamb inside.

Leftovers

Köfte Wraps: Slice leftover köfte and tuck them into warm pita or flatbread with some fresh greens, sliced tomatoes, and a drizzle of the yogurt sauce. You can also add a splash of hot sauce for extra flavor.

Köfte Salad: Crumble leftover köfte over a bed of mixed greens, cucumbers, cherry tomatoes, and red onions. Top with the yogurt sauce as a dressing or a simple lemon-olive oil vinaigrette for a hearty salad.

Köfte Rice Bowl: Serve the leftover köfte over a bowl of warm rice or bulgur. Add some roasted vegetables, a handful of fresh herbs, and a dollop of yogurt sauce for a quick and satisfying meal.

Mediterranean Pizza: Slice the leftover köfte thinly and use them as a topping for a homemade pizza. Add some olives, feta cheese, and fresh tomatoes for a Mediterranean twist.

Cooking Together

Timing the Köfte: When cooking köfte together, coordinate your timing so that both the patties and the yogurt sauce are ready simultaneously. While one person grills or pan-fries the köfte, the other can prepare the yogurt sauce and any additional sides or garnishes. This helps in keeping everything fresh and hot.

Ingredient Prep Relay: Divide the tasks of chopping herbs, mixing spices, and preparing the yogurt sauce. Set up a mini "prep station" for each task and then switch roles. This not only speeds up the process but also ensures everyone is involved in creating the dish.

Cooking Quiz: Test each other's knowledge about Turkish cuisine or other favorite foods while cooking. For example, you could quiz each other on the origins of different dishes or the ingredients used in traditional recipes.

MAIN COURSES

One-Pan Chicken with Apricots and Almonds

One-pan meals are my absolute favorite, especially when they deliver the kind of rich, complex flavors that make it seem like you've spent hours laboring in the kitchen.

This One-Pan Chicken with Apricots and Almonds is a perfect example. It tastes luxurious and indulgent, but the truth is, it's incredibly easy and effortless to make. The secret lies in the blend of warm spices—cumin and cinnamon—that infuse the chicken with deep, aromatic flavors in just a short amount of time.

I've always been a fan of chicken thighs, and this recipe is a testament to why they're such an underrated cut. They're juicy, flavorful, and perfectly suited to absorb all the wonderful spices in this dish. Plus, they're budget-friendly and always easy to find at the grocery store.

What really takes this dish to the next level, though, is the addition of dried apricots and toasted almonds. There's something about the combination of sweet, tangy fruit and crunchy nuts that feels incredibly luxurious, yet it's all done in a way that's surprisingly wallet-friendly.

This recipe is proof that you don't need to break the bank to create a meal that's both elegant and satisfying.

So, the next time you're craving something that feels a little more special but don't want to spend all day in the kitchen, give this one-pan wonder a try. It's a dish that will make you look like a culinary master without the fuss.

Ingredients For Two

- 2 bone-in, skin-on chicken thighs
- 1 teaspoon ground cumin
- 1/2 teaspoon ground cinnamon
- Salt and pepper, to taste
- 1 tablespoon extra virgin olive oil
- 1 small onion, thinly sliced
- 2 cloves garlic, minced
- 1/4 cup chicken broth or water
- 1/4 cup dried apricots, halved
- 1 tablespoon honey
- 1/4 cup toasted almonds, roughly chopped
- Fresh parsley or cilantro, for garnish (optional)

Prepare Time:
10 minutes

Cook Time:
35 minutes

Total Time:
45 minutes

Serving:
2

Instructions

- Pat the chicken thighs dry with a paper towel. Season both sides with cumin, cinnamon, and salt, and pepper to taste.

- Heat the olive oil in a large skillet over medium-high heat. Once hot, add the chicken thighs skin-side down. Cook for 5-7 minutes until the skin is golden and crispy. Flip the chicken and cook for another 2-3 minutes.

- Remove the chicken from the skillet and set aside.

- In the same skillet, add the sliced onions and garlic. Sauté for 3-4 minutes until the onions are softened and slightly caramelized.

- Pour in the chicken broth (or water) to deglaze the pan, scraping up any browned bits from the bottom. Add the dried apricots and honey, stirring to combine. Let the mixture come to a simmer.

- Return the chicken thighs to the skillet, skin-side up, nestling them into the apricot mixture. Reduce the heat to low, cover the skillet, and cook for 20-25 minutes, or until the chicken is cooked through and the apricots are tender.

- Once the chicken is done, sprinkle the toasted almonds over the top. Cook uncovered for an additional 2-3 minutes to allow the sauce to thicken slightly.

- Plate the chicken thighs with the apricot sauce spooned over them. Garnish with fresh parsley or cilantro if desired. Serve warm, with a side of crusty bread or rice to soak up the delicious sauce.

Tried & True Tips & Hacks

Sear for Flavor: Don't rush the searing process! Allow the chicken thighs to develop a deep, golden-brown crust before flipping. This step locks in the juices and adds a rich depth of flavor to the dish.

Use Bone-In, Skin-On Chicken: Bone-in, skin-on thighs bring more flavor and moisture to the dish, and the skin crisps up beautifully, adding texture. If you only have boneless, skinless thighs, reduce the cooking time slightly to avoid drying out the meat.

Spice it Up: Feel free to adjust the spices to your taste. If you like a bit of heat, add a pinch of cayenne pepper or paprika. The cumin and cinnamon are essential, but you can also experiment with other warm spices like coriander or turmeric.

Customize Your Dried Fruit: If apricots aren't your favorite, you can swap them out for other dried fruits like prunes, dates, or even raisins. They'll still provide that sweet contrast to the savory chicken.

Make Ahead: This dish tastes even better the next day as the flavors have more time to meld together. Prepare it a day ahead and reheat for a quick, flavorful meal.

Thicken the Sauce: If the sauce is too thin after cooking, remove the chicken and simmer the sauce uncovered for a few more minutes until it thickens to your desired consistency.

Serving Suggestions: Serve the dish with a side of couscous, rice, or a warm piece of flatbread to soak up the delicious sauce. Adding a dollop of yogurt on the side can also complement the spices wonderfully.

Toast Your Nuts: Always toast the almonds before adding them to the dish. This enhances their flavor and adds a perfect crunch to each bite.

Don't Overcrowd the Pan: Make sure not to overcrowd the skillet when searing the chicken. If necessary, sear the chicken in batches to ensure each piece gets a nice crust.

Use a Cast Iron Skillet: A heavy-bottomed pan like a cast iron skillet retains heat well and helps in developing a perfect sear on the chicken while evenly cooking everything.

Leftovers

Chicken Thighs: Shred any leftover chicken and use it in sandwiches, wraps, or salads the next day. It's especially delicious in a wrap with some fresh greens, a drizzle of the leftover sauce, and a bit of yogurt.

Apricots and Almonds: Leftover apricots can be chopped up and added to your morning oatmeal or yogurt for a sweet start to the day. Toasted almonds can be used as a topping for salads or desserts or mixed into granola.

Sauce: The leftover sauce from the dish can be repurposed as a flavorful base for soups or stews. You can also drizzle it over roasted vegetables or grains like couscous or quinoa.

Rice or Couscous: If you served the dish with rice or couscous, mix the leftovers with the remaining sauce and chicken for a quick and easy lunch the next day. This combination also works well as a stuffing for bell peppers.

Nuts in Baking: Leftover toasted almonds can be incorporated into baking recipes, such as muffins, cookies, or even as a crunchy topping for cakes and tarts.

Dried Fruit in Desserts: Use the remaining dried apricots in dessert recipes like fruit compotes, tarts, or mixed into batter for cakes and bread.

Spice Mix: If you mixed more spices than needed, save the blend in a jar and use it for other recipes. This spice mix works great with roasted vegetables, other meat dishes, or even sprinkled over popcorn for a savory snack.

Next Day Dinner: Transform the leftovers into a hearty grain bowl by layering the chicken, sauce, nuts, and dried fruits over a bed of cooked farro, bulgur, or brown rice. Add some fresh herbs or a squeeze of lemon juice to brighten the flavors.

Chicken Salad: Mix leftover chicken with a bit of mayonnaise, chopped celery, and a handful of the remaining toasted almonds for a quick and tasty chicken salad. Serve it on a sandwich, with crackers, or over greens.

Phyllo Pastry Filling: Chop the leftover chicken and mix it with some of the apricots and almonds. Use this mixture as a filling for phyllo pastry parcels for an easy, handheld lunch or snack.

Cooking Together

Prep and Chat: Start by prepping the ingredients together. While slicing the onions and mincing the garlic, enjoy a casual conversation or share stories. Cooking is a great way to bond, and prepping together helps set a relaxed and collaborative tone for the meal.

Sear with Teamwork: When it's time to sear the chicken, one person can handle the skillet while the other seasons and preps the apricots and almonds. This way, you can keep the cooking process smooth and efficient, making the task feel less like a chore and more like a shared experience.

Experiment with Spices: Make the seasoning process fun by experimenting with different spice levels. One person can mix the spices while the other tastes and adjusts. It's a great opportunity to explore flavors together and learn more about each other's taste preferences.

Timing is Key: Use the cooking time as a chance to discuss how the dish is coming along. While the chicken is simmering, plan out side dishes or dessert, or simply enjoy each other's company. Having a sense of how the meal is progressing adds to the enjoyment of the process.

Make it a Meal: When the dish is almost ready, work together to prepare a side or accompaniments. Whether it's cooking rice, setting the table, or making a quick salad, collaborating on the entire meal makes it feel more special and ensures everything is ready at the same time.

Clean Up Together: After enjoying the meal, make cleaning up part of the experience. One person can wash dishes while the other dries or tackle the cleanup together. It's a way to wrap up your cooking adventure and makes the whole experience feel more cooperative and less of a chore.

Clean Up Together: After enjoying the meal, make cleaning up part of the experience. One person can wash dishes while the other dries or tackle the cleanup together. It's a way to wrap up your cooking adventure and makes the whole experience feel more cooperative and less of a chore.

Create a Cooking Playlist: Curate a playlist of your favorite songs, or try some Turkish music to set the mood while you cook. Music can make the cooking process more enjoyable and create a relaxed, festive atmosphere.

Share the Experience: Take time to sit down and enjoy the meal together. Reflect on the cooking process, share your favorite parts, and discuss any new techniques you tried. Celebrating the effort you put into the meal makes the experience even more rewarding.

DESSERT

Muhallebi (Turkish Milk Pudding)

If there's an adult, sophisticated version of a pudding, this is it. Muhallebi, the Turkish milk pudding, has been a cherished treat in my life, though my childhood memories of it were a bit more colorful—literally. Back then, I enjoyed it drenched in grenadine syrup, which turned my tongue a vibrant shade of purplish red and left me feeling utterly satisfied and content.

This refined version of Muhallebi, however, is a delicate upgrade that brings a touch of elegance to this nostalgic dessert. Infused with rosewater, it introduces a subtle floral note that elevates the pudding to a level of sophistication perfect for adult tastes. Rosewater adds a layer of sophistication, which is my official excuse to indulge in this dessert as an adult and feel absolutely good about it.

Each spoonful of this creamy, light pudding is a reminder of the simple pleasures of childhood, now dressed up for grown-up palates. I promise, with its delicate fragrance and rich yet light texture, you'll find yourself falling in love with this sophisticated take on a classic. Enjoy it as a refined finale to any meal, and let it transport you to a place of elegant Turkish nostalgia.

Ingredients For Two

- 2 tablespoons cornstarch
- 1 cup whole milk, divided
- 1/4 cup granulated sugar
- 1/2 teaspoon rosewater
- 1/4 teaspoon vanilla extract
- 2 tablespoons crushed pistachios, for topping

Prepare Time:
10 minutes

Cook Time:
10 minutes

Total Time:
2 hours 20 minutes
(including chilling time)

Serving:
2

Instructions

- In a small bowl, dissolve the cornstarch in 2 tablespoons of cold milk to make a slurry. Stir until smooth.

- In a medium saucepan, combine the rest of the milk and sugar. Heat over medium heat, stirring occasionally until the sugar is fully dissolved and the mixture is warm.

- Gradually whisk the cornstarch slurry into the warm milk mixture. Continue to cook over medium heat, stirring constantly. Bring the mixture to a gentle simmer and cook until it thickens to a pudding-like consistency, about 5-7 minutes.

- Remove the saucepan from the heat. Stir in the rosewater and vanilla extract. Mix until evenly distributed.

- Pour the pudding into two small serving dishes or ramekins. Allow it to cool slightly at room temperature, then refrigerate for at least 2 hours or until fully chilled and set.

- Before serving, sprinkle the crushed pistachios on top of each pudding.

Tried & True Tips & Hacks

Perfect Consistency: Ensure you stir the mixture constantly while cooking to prevent lumps. If you notice any lumps forming, whisk vigorously or use a blender to smooth out the pudding before it sets.

Rosewater Caution: A little goes a long way with rosewater. Start with less and taste as you go to avoid overpowering the pudding. You can always add more if needed, but you can't take it out once it's mixed in.

Cornstarch Mixing: To avoid lumps from the cornstarch, always dissolve it in a small amount of cold milk before adding it to the warm mixture. This slurry method ensures a smooth and creamy texture.

Chilling Time: Allow the pudding to chill in the refrigerator for at least 2 hours to achieve the right consistency. If you're short on time, you can speed up the process by placing the dishes in a shallow ice bath before refrigerating.

Pistachio Prep: Toast the pistachios lightly in a dry skillet over medium heat for a few minutes before crushing them. This enhances their flavor and adds a delightful crunch to the pudding.

Serving Variations: For a creative twist, try adding a drizzle of honey or a sprinkle of ground cinnamon on top of the pudding along with the pistachios. This adds additional layers of flavor and makes the presentation more appealing.

Avoiding Skin Formation: To prevent a skin from forming on the surface of the pudding as it chills, cover the dishes with plastic wrap, pressing it gently against the surface of the pudding. This keeps the surface smooth and creamy.

Make Ahead: Muhallebi can be made a day in advance, making it a great option for entertaining or preparing ahead of time. Just keep it covered in the refrigerator until you're ready to serve.

Substitute Options: If you can't find rosewater, you can use a small amount of vanilla extract for a different but still delightful flavor. Alternatively, a hint of orange blossom water can also work well.

Texture Check: If the pudding seems too thick after chilling, whisk in a small amount of milk to loosen it up. This can help achieve the perfect creamy consistency without compromising the flavor.

Leftovers

Milk Pudding Uses: If you have leftover Muhallebi, it can be repurposed in a few creative ways. Use it as a creamy filling for pastries or layered desserts, such as trifles or parfaits. Simply spoon it into a glass or bowl, layer with fruit or granola, and enjoy.

Smoothie Addition: Blend leftover pudding with some milk or yogurt and fresh fruit to create a rich, creamy smoothie. This adds a touch of sweetness and silkiness to your drink, making for a super cool treat.

Pancake Topping: Use the leftover pudding as a decadent topping for pancakes or waffles. Warm it slightly and drizzle over your breakfast for an extra special start to your day.

Cake Filling: Incorporate leftover Muhallebi as a filling for cakes or cupcakes. It works well as a layer between cake slices or as a surprise filling in cupcakes, adding a touch of creamy sweetness.

Frozen Treats: Freeze the pudding in an ice cube tray or silicone molds to create pudding bites or popsicles. This can be a refreshing snack or dessert, especially during warmer months.

Yogurt Mix-In: Stir leftover pudding into plain yogurt for a flavorful twist. This combination makes for a tasty and creamy snack or breakfast option with a hint of rosewater and pistachio.

Crepe Filling: Spread leftover pudding inside crepes and fold or roll them up for a quick and delicious dessert. Add fresh fruit or a sprinkle of nuts on top for extra flavor.

Dessert Sauce: Thin out the pudding with a bit of milk or cream and use it as a sauce for fruit or baked goods. It can be drizzled over fresh berries, baked apples, or even a slice of cake.

Cottage Cheese Blend: Mix leftover pudding with cottage cheese for a creamy and slightly tangy dessert option. This adds a different texture and flavor profile while still keeping the pudding's essence.

Garnished Fruit Salad: Use the pudding as a creamy dressing for a fruit salad. Fold it into a mix of your favorite fruits for a luscious, pudding-coated fruit salad that feels like a dessert.

Cooking Together

Prep and Share: Begin by preparing the Muhallebi together. As you measure out the ingredients and stir the pudding mixture, take this opportunity to chat about each other's favorite desserts from childhood. Sharing personal stories can make the cooking experience more enjoyable and personal.

Cultural Insights: As you wait for the pudding to chill, dive into a conversation about cultural food traditions. Discuss why certain foods are cherished in your backgrounds and any interesting food customs you've encountered. For instance, you might talk about how the symbolism of pomegranates in Turkish cuisine ties into cultural beliefs and practices.

Traditional vs. Modern: Reflect on how traditional recipes have evolved over time. Talk about how modern adaptations, like using rosewater instead of more traditional ingredients, bridge the gap between classic and contemporary tastes. This could also lead to a discussion about how global influences are reshaping traditional dishes.

Share Experiences: Discuss the process of making food from scratch versus buying ready-made products. Explore how cooking methods and ingredient choices reflect personal and cultural values. This can lead to a broader conversation about the importance of homemade meals and the joy of cooking together.

Cooking Traditions: Share how different cultures approach cooking and meal preparation. Compare how cooking is done in various parts of the world and how certain practices, like communal cooking or specific meal times, reflect cultural values and social norms.

DRINK
Turkish Mint Lemonade

This Turkish Mint Lemonade is a smart (and by smart, I mean brilliant) choice for those who crave the joy of a special drink at the end of a meal but prefer to steer clear of alcohol. It's like a classic mocktail that was enjoying a rich tradition in Turkey long before the term "mocktail" ever hit the Instagram scene. This refreshing beverage is a testament to how simple, fresh ingredients can elevate a drink to something extraordinary.

And I must admit that when I'm in the mood to skip dessert but still want a satisfying finish to my meal, this lemonade comes to the rescue. It offers a perfectly balanced blend of sweetness, tartness, and the invigorating flavor of mint, making it a gratifying alternative to heavier desserts (apologies Kunefe and Turkish Tulumba, you still hold a place in my heart). The combination of freshly squeezed lemon juice with a hint of mint and just the right amount of sugar creates a drink that feels both indulgent and refreshing.

It's the kind of drink that feels like a treat yet doesn't weigh you down. Each sip provides a burst of citrusy freshness and aromatic mint, leaving you feeling content and rejuvenated. Whether you're looking to end a meal on a high note or simply enjoy a flavorful beverage, this Turkish Mint Lemonade is a sophisticated choice that doesn't compromise on enjoyment.

Ingredients For Two

- 1/4 cup water (for dissolving sugar)
- 1/4 cup granulated sugar (adjust to taste)
- A handful of fresh mint leaves (about 10-12 leaves)
- 1/2 cup freshly squeezed lemon juice (about 2 large lemons)
- 1 cup cold water (or sparkling water for a fizzy version)
- Ice cubes (as needed)
- Lemon slices and mint sprigs (for garnish)

✅ **Prepare Time:**
10 minutes

✅ **Total Time:**
10 minutes (excluding cooling time for the syrup)

✅ **Serving:**
2 (Makes 2 glasses)

Instructions

- In a small saucepan, combine the 1/4 cup of water with the granulated sugar. Heat over medium heat, stirring until the sugar is completely dissolved.

- Add the mint leaves to the saucepan and let them steep in the syrup for about 5 minutes. Remove from heat and let it cool completely.

- In a pitcher, combine the freshly squeezed lemon juice with the cooled mint syrup. Stir well to mix the flavors.

- Add 1 cup of cold water to the pitcher. If you prefer a fizzy lemonade, substitute this with sparkling water. Stir to combine.

- Fill glasses with ice cubes and pour the lemonade over the ice. Garnish with lemon slices and mint sprigs.

- Taste and adjust sweetness if needed by adding more sugar or more lemon juice as per your preference.

- Serve immediately for the best flavor and freshness.

Tried & True Tips & Hacks

Lemon Juice Hack: To get the most juice out of your lemons, roll them firmly on the countertop before cutting and juicing. This helps release more juice.

Mint Freshness: For the most vibrant mint flavor, gently bruise the mint leaves before adding them to the syrup. This releases more of the mint's essential oils.

Adjust Sweetness: Taste your lemonade before serving. If it's too tart, add a little more sugar or honey to balance the flavors. Conversely, if it's too sweet, add a splash more lemon juice.

Mint Infusion: For a stronger mint flavor, you can steep additional mint leaves directly in the lemonade after it's mixed. Just remove the leaves before serving to avoid bitterness.

Chill Thoroughly: To ensure your lemonade is as refreshing as possible, chill it in the refrigerator for at least an hour before serving. This allows the flavors to meld together and the drink to be properly cool.

Sparkling Twist: If you prefer a fizzy version, substitute the cold water with sparkling water. For extra effervescence, add a splash of soda right before serving to keep the bubbles lively.

Garnish Ideas: Enhance the presentation by adding extra mint sprigs or lemon slices to each glass. You can also freeze mint leaves or lemon slices in ice cubes for a beautiful and functional garnish.

Batch Preparation: Make a larger batch of the mint syrup ahead of time and store it in the refrigerator for up to a week. You can quickly mix it with lemon juice and water whenever you're in the mood for a refreshing drink.

Sweetener Alternatives: If you prefer a healthier option, use honey or agave syrup instead of granulated sugar. Adjust the quantity to taste, as these alternatives can be sweeter than regular sugar.

Herbal Variations: Experiment with other herbs like basil or thyme for a unique twist. Just follow the same process you would with mint, adjusting to taste.

Flavor Boosters: Add a splash of fruit juice (like raspberry or strawberry) for a fruity twist. Mix it in when combining the lemon juice and mint syrup for an extra layer of flavor.

Serving Tips: Serve the lemonade in chilled glasses to keep it cooler longer. If you're making it for a gathering instead of a party of two, consider preparing it in a large pitcher with ice to serve a crowd.

Leftovers

Lemon Juice

Make Lemon Ice Cubes: Freeze any leftover lemon juice in ice cube trays. These can be used to cool down and add a burst of lemon flavor to future beverages.

Use in Cooking: Incorporate leftover lemon juice into salad dressings, marinades, or even in baked goods for a zesty kick.

Mint Leaves

Mint-Infused Water: Add leftover mint leaves to a pitcher of water for a refreshing infused drink.

Mint Tea: Steep leftover mint leaves in hot water to make a soothing herbal tea. Sweeten with honey or a splash of lemon juice if desired.

Flavor Enhancer: Use the mint in other dishes like tabbouleh or yogurt sauces for an added burst of freshness.

Mint Syrup

Cocktails & Mocktails: Use the mint syrup in other beverages such as mojitos (alcoholic or non-alcoholic) or any other mocktails.

Desserts: Drizzle the syrup over ice cream, yogurt, or fruit salads for added sweetness and a minty twist.

Marinades: Incorporate the syrup into marinades for chicken or pork to add a hint of sweetness and mint flavor.

Leftover Beverage

Ice Pops: Pour any leftover lemonade into ice pop molds and freeze for a refreshing treat.

Cocktail Mixer: Use leftover lemonade as a base for cocktails or as a mixer for sparkling wines.

Refrigerate: Store any leftover lemonade in a tightly sealed pitcher or bottle in the refrigerator. It should stay fresh for up to 3 days.

Avoid Dilution: To prevent the lemonade from becoming too diluted, keep any ice cubes separate and add them just before serving.

Cooking Together:

Discuss Traditions: While preparing the lemonade, take the opportunity to discuss the cultural significance of mint and lemon in Turkish cuisine. Share any personal experiences or stories related to these ingredients.

Explore Ingredients: Talk about other traditional Turkish beverages or dishes you might want to try together and how different flavors and ingredients contribute to the rich tapestry of Turkish cuisine.

Create a Beverage Bar: Set up a small beverage station with different garnishes and flavorings. You can each create your own customized versions of the lemonade, adding your favorite extras.

Make it a Habit: Use this time to plan future meals and drinks together. Discuss how you might use leftover lemonade or mint syrup in other recipes, and share ideas for incorporating these ingredients into different dishes.

Share Traditions: Share any personal or family traditions related to food and drink and compare them with Turkish customs. This can lead to interesting conversations and a deeper appreciation of different cultures.

Share Memories: While enjoying the Turkish Mint Lemonade, take turns sharing favorite drinks from your childhood or travels. Discuss how these beverages made you feel and any special memories associated with them.

Compare and Contrast: Compare your favorite childhood drinks or travel beverages with the Turkish Mint Lemonade. Talk about how different cultures and personal experiences influence the drinks you love.

Inspiration for Future Recipes: Use this discussion to inspire future cooking adventures. Maybe you'll want to recreate a favorite childhood drink or explore a beverage from a memorable trip, incorporating the same sense of enjoyment and discovery into your next culinary project.

IN CONCLUSION...

Mediterranean Escapes Have No Real End

As you reach the end of this journey through Mediterranean cooking for two, and I hope you feel the same warmth and joy that inspired every recipe and story in this book. Each dish reflects my deep love for the Mediterranean, blending simplicity with flavor to create manageable recipes for two. This book is more than just a collection of recipes; it's a celebration of the Mediterranean way of life—where food is not just about nourishment but about connection, tradition, and a touch of magic.

In crafting these recipes, I aimed to honor the essence of Mediterranean cuisine while keeping sustainability and zero waste at the forefront. Every ingredient, every technique was chosen to minimize waste and maximize flavor, creating meals that are not only delicious but also mindful of our environment. My goal was to bring together all the elements I cherish about Mediterranean cooking and see what happens when they come together. What happened is the book you're now reading, filled with dishes that transport you across the Mediterranean from the comfort of your own kitchen.

Cooking is a sensory experience that can whisk you away to distant lands without needing to board an airplane. Yet, if these recipes ignite a spark of wanderlust and inspire you to visit the Mediterranean in person, then I consider this book a success in many wonderful ways.

Thank you for joining me on this culinary adventure. May your kitchen be filled with the aromas of the Mediterranean, and may every meal you prepare bring a little piece of this vibrant and diverse region into your home. Happy cooking and bon appétit!

Made in United States
Troutdale, OR
02/08/2025

28708202R00060